THE
SEVEN
VICTORIES
OF THE
DIVINE CHILD

Claiming Your Divine Inheritance

MICHAEL JONES

Spirit Source Publishing
South Bend, Indiana

Library of Congress   2011912814

ISBN 978-0-9837780-1-1

Cover Art and Design: 1106 Design, LLC
Book Design and Layout: 1106 Design, LLC
Editing: Stephanie Gunning

Spirit Source Publishing
P.O. Box 8181
South Bend, IN. 46660
Website: www.MySpiritSource.net
Email: info@MySpiritSource.net

Dedication

To my amazing and tireless supporter, best friend and beloved, Kathy; through your encouragement and confidence, I was given the strength to keep moving forward with this book.

To my children, Elizabeth (Liz), Alex and Abram. I love you and I am blessed to have you in my life.

To my dad, Herbert, for your love, and for leading by example.

In loving memory of my mom, Louise (Lou), for her ongoing interest in these teachings.

"*The offering of wisdom is better than any material offering;*
for the goal of all work is spiritual wisdom."
—Bhagavad Gita 4:33

Contents

Contents

Acknowledgments

I AM GRATEFUL TO ALL of my earthly teachers, who are too numerous to mention individually, though I am confident that you know who you are.

Let me also extend my thanks to my spiritual teachers and beloved friends, Dr. Robert Johnson and Jewels. You have been instrumental, directly and indirectly, in assisting in the manifestation of these teachings. I am forever thankful to our Father/Mother God for answering my prayers with your presence.

Thanks also to the three mentors I have been gifted with in this lifetime: Herbert Jones, Randy Bibler, and David Kreager. You have taught me more than each of you will ever fully realize.

I would like to acknowledge my insightfully brilliant editor, Stephanie Gunning, for her patience, hard work and intuitive knowing.

Introduction

"We can build giant bridges to span rivers of monstrous width, but we are unable to span the simple question of 'Who am I?'"
—Paul Brunton, *The Secret Path*

MORE AND MORE PEOPLE are seeking to understand spiritual truth. They want clarity about their purpose in life, and to develop a deeper connection to God. *The Seven Victories of the Divine Child: Claiming Your Divine Inheritance* offers you insight into one path to God's Kingdom, one path allowing you to claim your birthright as a spiritual being.

The fact that you are reading this book suggests that there is something in the message of the title and subtitle that appeals to you. In the spiritual quest to quench the thirst born deep within them to regain closeness with God, people are often drawn to explore various religions and their sacred texts, metaphysics, and philosophy. People often hop from one topic or area of study to another without fully understanding what drives their search. Whether or not they are conscious of it, the internal drive of a seeker is the result of asking self-imposed questions.

1

Seeking begins by having confusion about life and the spiritual realm or experiencing things we've not been able to reconcile. The yearning for answers is often heightened after we've experienced some painful event in our lives. One positive outcome of pain is that it appears to split us wide open in such a way that it opens the door for us to strive to gain some real, deeper meaning of God and Spirit.

Regardless of the catalyst, I find nothing of concern underlying all of the seeking, except not having a degree of clarity on what we are really looking for. Underneath all seeking, at the core, are two primary things:

1. Desire to find an answer to the question, "Who am I?"
2. A deep-seated desire to regain oneness with God.

Spirit and spirituality are universal. They unite the spiritual family of humanity. In practice, spirituality does not divide people as many traditional modern-day religions appear to do. When modern-day religions divide humanity, it is nothing short of primitive child's play in the eyes of universal spirituality.

Let me be clear. I am not saying that modern-day religion is bad. Just that a vast majority of religions have veered into the weeds and away from the path of the teachings brought forward by their original spiritual leaders. Far too much emphasis has been placed on trying to prove another religion wrong or convert someone to a particular way of believing. Looking at the world around us, it is self-evident that the current ways are simply not working.

I am here as a messenger to share a message with you that does not relate exclusively to one religion. These teachings come from Spirit flowing through me, as well as from me. I offer them freely to you for your consideration. This book contains a message for you no matter where you are starting from, and it has the potential to assist you in taking significant steps on the path of your spiritual growth and discovery.

Introduction

If you choose to apply these teachings to your life, the benefits that you'll experience will be profound and real. When we, as individuals, take personal responsibility for our spirituality, the blessings are almost too numerous to mention. To be a Divine Child is your birthright. Having said that, here are some of the ways that you will benefit from the teachings found in this book and from claiming your divine inheritance. You will learn to:

- Personally experience the peaceful bliss of God's presence here and now.
- Attune to the still, small voice of divine guidance within you, and allow it to positively influence you in all matters—both the material and the spiritual.
- Understand and learn how to utilize the principles of cause and effect, abundance, health, and happiness.
- Extinguish feelings of fear, anxiety, and nervous tension, and infuse your personal relationships and career with a sense of purpose and fulfillment.
- Let go of reactionary habits and judgments, thus eliminating internal conflicts and living your life authentically.

Without a doubt, I am confident that you will personally benefit in many, many more ways than the few listed here. Remember, you are a Divine Child of God and this is your inheritance. I am excited for you as you progress on your path towards higher consciousness and renewed perceptions of who you really are!

My only request of you, dear reader, is that you give yourself the gift of having an open heart and an open mind as you progress through these pages. *The Seven Victories of the Divine Child* is a modern-day revelation, pointing your way to, and through the doorway of higher consciousness. The perceptions gained through careful study of this material offer profound, positive, life-changing effects for the spiritual aspirant.

What You Are About to Experience

As you read, you will likely have an experience similar to what is described in *The Gospel of Thomas* (saying 2). *The Gospel of Thomas* is a collection of 113 sayings. This gospel was not included in the canon with the twenty-seven writings that now make up the New Testament. *The Gospel of Thomas* was lost and then rediscovered in Egypt in 1945 (along with over fifty other early Christian texts), and are considered Gnostic writings.

> *Jesus said, Let him who seeks continue seeking until he finds. When he finds, he will become troubled. When he becomes troubled, he will be astonished, and he will rule over all.*

This passage from *The Gospel of Thomas* (HarperCollins, 1990) is fitting to introduce this book. It may well outline the phases you'll go through as you read. It could be that in one way or another you are seeking a closer relationship with God. And in seeking such a relationship, you may intuitively know that there is a path to follow that will lead you, a Divine Child, home to God's Kingdom, which is your true and original home.

You may become troubled by your initial findings. Troubled in the sense that you may see and learn things quite different than what you once thought, or were told. Next, your concern could turn into astonishment. This change could come to you as a feeling or an awakened awareness deep within you. At some level, you may feel like you have always known this information. You may feel as if a fog has been lifted from your field of vision.

You will find that the insights and perspectives offered in this work do not run against the grain of most organized religions. In fact, they may very well pull together some silver threads of truth that run through many religions. You will find some spiritual truths brought into focus that, up until now, you have been unable to reconcile. Now is the time to piece together a spiritual puzzle. When the pieces of the puzzle are applied to everyday life, they will aid your soul on its journey, and the peace that passes all understanding will surround and enfold you.

How I Came to These Realizations

As a child, I attended a Catholic Church in my family's community. Looking back, I experienced an interesting combination of religious and spiritual upbringing. On one hand, there was my mother, who grew up in the Catholic faith and was the driver behind attending these services. On the other hand, there was my dad, who embraced a larger universal spiritual experience of this life and of the spirit world beyond.

I liked aspects of the Catholic service. I found many of the rituals quite beautiful. However, I found many of the Catholic Church's outlooks and beliefs limiting, and the services always left me wanting more. I did not feel any closer to God as a result of those experiences. I often felt myself wondering (and doubting) whether the Church's current practices accurately reflected the original teachings of Jesus. (As you read on, you will answer for yourself whether they do or not.) I felt what I was learning at the time just scratched the surface of deeper spiritual wisdom that was available. Although I am no longer a practicing Catholic, I am grateful for the experiences I had in the Church.

I was still a teenager when I began to develop a clearer, more expanded view of God, Jesus the Christ, and the idea of oneness with God. As my development progressed, the scriptures began to take on a new, more personal meaning connected with my soul.

In my early twenties, my spiritual growth and beliefs did not fit nicely into any particular religious group—or so I thought. My spirituality was becoming universal in nature. I was learning that there were threads of truth woven into the fabric of all the world's religions. Fitting squarely within one particular faith tradition did not offer my soul peace. Embracing universal spirituality did (and still does).

I believed then, as now, that it is just as Pierre Teilhard de Chardin first said: We are all spiritual beings having a human experience, as opposed to human beings seeking to catch an occasional spiritual experience. Believing that we are spiritual beings drives my heart and soul to understand and connect, in a meaningful way, with the spiritual side of life. After all, God is Spirit.

As my spiritual growth continued and my awareness expanded, I felt I had rediscovered the core of my being rather than discovered something new. It had always been there, but I'd lost it somewhere. I am sure that through grace, realization of oneness with God could happen all at once for someone. But for me, it was a gradual process of rediscovery.

When I kept an open mind and perspective, I was led to read sacred scriptures from different world religions and other books of spiritual wisdom, learn from them, apply the information, and experience the beauty of the principles in action in my life. Studying universal spirituality from different and unfamiliar sources helped me reconcile many of the conflicts and incongruities I'd noticed in the spiritual tenets I had been taught.

Learning spiritual insights from different traditions has been, and continues to be, a great gift—one that I wish to share with you. I believe that many of the pieces of your spiritual puzzle will come into focus for you as well, as you study universal wisdom.

About this Book

The Seven Victories of the Divine Child is organized in six parts. Part One, "Redefining Our Perspective of God and the Universal Divine Child," will provide you with a new perspective on God, the nature of his Universal Divine Child, and the Kingdom of God. It describes how your beliefs influence your perception of everything, including the spirit world, God, and God's Kingdom. If you are to become aware of God, not just "believe" in God, but really experience God, you must be willing to allow your perceptions of God to shift and grow in a way that will allow you to move in the direction that masters of different traditions for millennia have taught us.

Part One, more so than any other part of this book, is heavily laden with sacred scriptural references. I predominantly refer to, and cite passages from *The Holy Bible, The Bhagavad Gita,* and *The Upanishads.* In doing so, I do not mean to imply that other sacred texts from outside of Christianity and Hinduism are not valuable. Part One lays the foundation for later discussions and helps bring the remainder of the book to life. Each subsequent part of the book is increasingly specific about how to bring universal spiritual principles into your everyday life.

Part Two, "Allow God to Guide You Each Step of the Way," describes how a person can get on a spiritual path, where to find the starting point, how to access higher consciousness and oneness with God while we are still on Earth in the physical body. Part Two describes the steps required to become more aware of God's presence and the connecting path to "hear" or "discern" his/her guidance each step of the way.

In this book, God is referred to as both Father and Mother, and sometimes as the Divine Parents, for God includes both masculine and feminine aspects. The Higher Self, called by many names, in many traditions, is our connection to the Divine Parents. Understanding and gaining access to perceive the Higher Self, its characteristics and attributes, helps us understand who we really are. You will gain an understanding of how to become more aware of, and connect with the Higher Self after reading Part Two.

Part Three, "Obstacles on the Path to Victory." It is invaluable to understand the obstacles on the path of the Divine Child explained in modern-day terms and examples. Understanding the Lower Self, its characteristics and attributes, helps us understand an important part of our nature as human beings. You will learn how your Lower Self acts as both friend and foe in your life. Understanding the Lower

Self and its purpose will open your eyes to why certain things happen the way they do. The Lower Self has several weapons in its arsenal.

In Part Three, we will explore proven methods to overcome the obstacles the Lower Self puts in your path. Armed with this knowledge, you will be able to move beyond the Lower Self and experience victory in expanding your consciousness and allowing the Higher Self to lead you to victory and oneness with God.

In Part Four, "Universal Wisdom Tools of the Divine Child," you will learn, or perhaps re-learn, the purpose and power of many ancient tools. These universal tools become most valuable when correctly applied to your life. Part Four will cover topics such as the power of thought and creative energy, the power of prayer (and what prayer really is), and the power and purpose of meditation, as well as the invaluable topic of self-mastery. All of the tools of the Divine Child are described in detail to serve as helpful aids as you work through life's battles and victories.

Part Five, "The Battles and Victories of the Divine Child," covers the challenges you must experience on the path to claim your divine inheritance. All sacred scriptures include descriptions of an epic battle of light versus darkness. Whether you realize it or not, there is a similar battle going on inside each of us all the time. We experience a tug-of-war between the Lower Self and the Higher Self on the battlefield of the soul. The definition of soul is the individual spirit when it's incarnated in a body.

In Part Five, you will learn about the seven battles and the seven victories everyone experiences in life. Valuable insights into the nature of the battles, along with tools and guidance on how to effectively use them to experience victory appear here.

Part Six, "Claiming Your Divine Inheritance," explains how the successful resolution of the battles between the Higher Self and the Lower Self is a conscious blending of the two Selves into one. Following union of the two Selves, and now led by the Higher Self, you will experience an understanding and realization of oneness with God.

The purpose of the book in its entirety is to demonstrate to you that we all truly can expand our conscious awareness, both in principle and in practice, of who we really are: Divine Children, sons and daughters of God.

Closing Thoughts

The Seven Victories of the Divine Child is written for people of all faiths and traditions, including those who are not yet sure what they believe. This book is a life manual of sorts; my intention is for there to be something here for everyone.

We all share an underlying commonality: We are spiritual beings living in a material world. A spiritual being housed within a human body, trying to live in the spiritual and material worlds at the same time, encounters common challenges. These challenges may appear quite different on the surface of each person's life, but there are commonalities that flow outward from our core beings. This work is about the process of overcoming those challenges and a process of becoming ever clearer reflections of who we really are.

We gain insight as we unravel key spiritual mysteries. Our insights allow us to see beyond the smoke and mirrors of our various life challenges. Armed with these insights, we are able to blend our true, spiritual being and our human being, into one.

The messages contained within these pages are dedicated to my spiritual brothers and sisters who feel the same stirring and longing deep within their souls as I do to understand their spiritual natures and deepen their relationship to our Mother/Father God. My sincere desire is to offer you the light of spiritual wisdom as you navigate your course through this lifetime. I wish you everything that honors your highest and best good.

In love and in light,
Michael

PART ONE

Redefining Our Perspective of God and the Universal Divine Child

Oh Father, in the past, I often pictured you high in heaven—far away—sitting on a throne watching over the world. I did not know how to talk to you. You seemed so distant and I seemed so low.

How I must have been asleep to think such thoughts. Through your grace and through truth, I now realize that you have been with me all along. You were so close that I could not see you. Your light, your life, is in and around everything—for all is in God and God is in all. From the butterfly, to the bird, to the deer, and to the man—your presence is alive in every atom and every cell of my being.

Father/Mother, thank you for your love, light and life. Thank you for awakening me from my sleep.

CHAPTER 1
Preparing Ourselves to Receive

"Empty yourself in order that you may receive."
—Unknown

OVER 2,000 YEARS AGO it is written that Master Jesus said the Kingdom of God is at hand. Yet today, it appears that the multitude is either no longer looking for the Kingdom, or doesn't know where and how to find it. Were Jesus's teachings flawed? Or have his teachings been misinterpreted and misunderstood for all these many years?

It is my viewpoint that Jesus's teachings (as well as the teachings of other masters) aren't flawed, but have been misinterpreted and misunderstood for centuries. The vast majority of people are caught up in looking for God and the Kingdom of God in the wrong place. What will it take for humanity to make the adjustment in perception necessary to be able to perceive the Kingdom of God while still on Earth?

We all long for understanding, meaning, and purpose in our lives. Today, more people than ever are experiencing a shift, an internal, almost magnetic pull toward deeper spiritual understanding and longing for closeness with God. Our answers for how to gain understanding, and experience meaning and purpose may be closer to us than we think.

As we begin our journey together, let us consider *The Gospel of Thomas* (saying 113), where Jesus speaks about the Kingdom of God:

> *When will the kingdom come? (Jesus said), It will not come by waiting for it. It will not be a matter of saying "here it is" or "there it is," Rather, the kingdom of the father is spread out upon the Earth and men do not see it.*

Are we still looking, still waiting for God's kingdom to come like people thousands of years ago? Or do we expect to experience the kingdom only after we pass away? If the Kingdom of God is spread out upon the earth and we do not see it, what will it take for us to see it? What needs to happen in our own perception and awareness for us to recognize it? The answers to these and other questions are the focus of this book.

Sometimes we seek spiritual guidance and answers, but we're not sure what we hope to find. However, if we pay attention, the soul acts as a compass of sorts. In combination with guidance from Spirit, it directs us to what we are here to do and experience. The soul is that part of us which is spirit incarnated in an individual body. Truly, the Divine Child longs for oneness with God; in seeking this out, it seeks to claim its divine inheritance. Traveling toward this destination, like many other journeys in life, can be a remarkable process.

Whether you are consciously searching for a deeper, closer, more meaningful connection with God, or guidance and answers to some of your life's current challenges, you will find much comfort and peace within these teachings. This book will offer you a framework to enter the Kingdom of God and claim your divine inheritance while still on Earth. But you will need to apply the teachings to your own life.

Your path to the Kingdom of God picks up from wherever you are today. There is no need to look for a starting point and the ending point will become clear.

Our Beliefs Influence Our Perceptions

Beliefs are very interesting. We often hold on to our beliefs as though they are prized possessions. The fact that we believe something to be a certain way, however, does not automatically make it true. Beliefs are often formed unconsciously and they're too seldom questioned. Our beliefs are largely a byproduct of our upbringing, meaning the geographic area where we grew up, what we have been taught, and our personal experiences.

You may find it beneficial to be reminded of a process the mind goes through when it is exposed to, and experiences, new or different information. New information is filtered through our current mental map of beliefs. This mental map has been formed by our life experiences, plus what we have read, heard, or been taught. When we encounter new or different information, it flows through the filter of our current mental map. We mentally review new information for potential conflicts (real or imagined) within the framework of our current beliefs. For many of us, much of this process happens unconsciously.

Be mindful about falling into this unconscious process. Unless you consciously choose to consider new information, your mind will search for past reference points and assumptions that support your current beliefs. As you read this book, you may find some of your current beliefs being challenged. You may have to think deeply to gain a clear picture. Do not be on autopilot, controlled only by your past mental map.

Here is one of the questions that are important for you to consider: What do you currently believe that no longer serves your highest good? This may be a difficult question to answer. Only you know (or can discover) the beliefs that best fit your life. Nonetheless, it's important to ask the question. Your beliefs influence your perceptions whether you're aware of this fact or not. Your beliefs and perceptions give everything in life meaning.

Here is an example of a *perception* to consider: My observation is that a vast majority of people continue to project human characteristics, qualities, and emotions onto God. The anthropomorphic view of God (for example, that God has human characteristics, such as anger, jealousy, and vengefulness) is none other than a concept of God created in a human image. Now is the time in our spiritual evolution and awareness to move beyond this primitive, elementary way of perceiving our all-loving God. How we perceive God has everything to do with how we will experience God's presence in our lives.

Our spiritual perceptions (meaning, our intuitive knowing) percolate to the surface of our awareness from a level beyond what we can perceive using the five physical senses. Our spiritual discernments unfold at our own pace and in perfect timing.

Unraveling Divine Mysteries

To make the crooked path to the Kingdom of God straight, our first few steps must involve exploring and, in some cases, unraveling several divine mysteries. The process of unlocking these beautiful divine mysteries allows our perceptions to become open to divine guidance. As we open ourselves up to divine guidance, we prepare ourselves to receive everything we need in perfect ways and under grace.

We'll consult several sacred scriptures in the process of unraveling their divine mysteries. Many beautiful texts are available for us to consider. It is interesting to me that few people take the time to read or study spiritual writings outside their chosen religions. Perhaps we would show more understanding for each other and engage in fewer wars and conflicts if we truly understood how many characteristics we share. Far too many people focus only on the differences between them. In reading texts from different traditions, we can begin to create greater harmony right away.

It appears that many religions teach only the basics in their public services. But all traditions have a deeper, more esoteric element to their teachings. This is where the deeper truths often lie. These esoteric elements generally are not taught to the masses. Exploring these "hidden" elements is where we are headed. In the next few chapters, we will discuss the esoteric elements of divine mysteries that most religions do not openly offer. As we shine the light on our deeper understanding of these "hidden" teachings, the clouds covering those truths will be lifted away.

The victories of the Divine Child begin as soon as we open up and allow our spiritual perceptions and awareness to move to the forefront of our minds. All we need to begin to accomplish this is *will* and *intention*. Our intention to be open prepares us to claim and receive our divine inheritance.

CHAPTER 2

Redefining Our Perspective of God and the Universal Divine Child

"The real voyage of discovery consists not in seeking new landscapes, but in having new eyes."
—Marcel Proust

A S A REFERENCE POINT, when quoting *The Holy Bible,* unless otherwise noted, I am using George M. Lamsa's translation of the Aramaic of the Peshitta, *The Holy Bible from the Ancient Eastern Text* (A.J. Holman, 1933). I am using Eknath Easwaran's translations of *The Bhagavad Gita* (The Blue Mountain Center of Meditation, 1985) and *The Upanishads* (The Blue Mountain Center of Meditation, 1987). Texts from the Nag Hammadi Library are drawn from *The Nag Hammadi Library in English* (HarperCollins Publishers, 1990), edited by James M. Robinson.

Hereafter, text set in [brackets] within a scriptural quotation has been added to clarify the esoteric meaning of the quotation.

Before the Creation of This World

It seems fitting to start at a recognizable beginning to build a common foundation for our understanding. I say *a* beginning because there have been other beginnings going back further in time than we can even begin to comprehend.

Before the beginning described in the creation story of the Bible, all existed in the mind of God. It was, and continues to be, the will of God to extend his/her thoughts through the levels of creation, first manifesting them as ideas from the unmanifested, then going down the vibrational ladder to where ideas manifest into the building blocks of matter. Most people would assume that because the Bible starts with *The Book of Genesis,* nothing existed prior to this beginning. Actually, nothing is said in the Bible about what existed *prior* to the beginning described in the story.

The building blocks of our material world (and universe) may have been manifested at the beginning of *Genesis.* But God, the eternal Spirit, existed beforehand. We know this because the first two verses of chapter 1 of *Genesis* use the terms "God created" and "the Spirit of God moved." If God, and the Spirit of God, were around *before* the beginning of the *Genesis* creation story, what or who else existed *before* the story begins?

One could say that there should be a chapter 0 of *Genesis.* Chapter 0 would contain insight into what precedes chapter 1. Let us just consider *some* of the information that *could* be written.

Genesis Chapter 0

God is eternal, everlasting—without a beginning and without an ending. God is the All in all. In reality, God is all that there is. Nothing exists outside of or apart from God. God is complete and lacks nothing.

God's vibratory thoughts and energy manifest from the unmanifested as Love, Light, and Life.

Through God's will, Love pours forth from God manifesting as the Holy Spirit of God. Through God's will, Light pours forth from God manifesting as the active intelligence of God. Through God's will, Life pours forth from God manifesting as pure awareness, and resulting in various levels of consciousness.

All three of these aspects of God—Love, Light, and Life—are at one with God, individual and distinct, yet with no separation from their source.

God, in an incomprehensible creative union with the Holy Spirit of God (Love), brought forth (or manifested, or begot) a Universal Divine Child. This Universal Divine Child, who people will call by many names, is a reflection of its Divine Parents. The Universal Divine Child is one with God, omnipresent in all of creation.

So it was, before the worlds and their heavens were formed, God the Father, God the Mother (the Holy Spirit of God or Love), and God the Universal Divine Child existed.

We catch a glimpse of *the beginnings* we seek, as they would be highlighted in our invented chapter 0, *before the worlds were formed,* in the following verse of *The Holy Bible* (John 17:5):

> *So now, O my Father, glorify me with thee, with the same glory which I* [the Universal Divine Child] *had with you before the world was made.*

A later beginning is referenced in *The Book of Genesis*. There, in chapter 1, verses 1–2, we read:

> *God created* [thought about and the thought manifested] *the heavens* [plural] *and the earth in the* [in this] *very beginning. And the earth was without form, and void; and darkness* [the lack of knowledge/ignorance] *was upon the face of the deep. And the Spirit of God moved upon the face of the water.*

We can assume the term "water" was used because either the Earth was without form (so "water" means space or reflective space) or "water" had been created in a prior manifestation. *Genesis* next reads (2–5):

> *And God said* [created a vibration with his thoughts or voice], *Let there be light; and there was light. And God saw that the light was good; and God separated the light from the darkness. And God called the light Day, and the darkness he called Night.*

This newly created *light* cannot be the type of light that emanates from the sun, because the sun, moon, and stars were created later—on the third day of creation—according to *Genesis* 1:13–18. So, if God had not yet created the sun to provide the light, what is the meaning of "light" created on the first day?

The creation of *light* on the first day will make more sense if you replace the word "light" with the word "intelligence." God first distilled intelligence into the very fabric of creation, into the basic building blocks of matter: atoms. The intelligence God built into atoms causes their vibration and movement. Intelligence is what makes atoms and their smaller components (electrons, protons, neutrons) behave as they do.

Moving forward to the so-called fifth day of creation, we read:

> *Then God said, Let us make man in our image, after our likeness; and let them have dominion over. ... So God created man in his own image, in the image of God he created him; male and female he created them.* (Genesis 1:26–27).

When God says, *"Let us make man in our image, after our likeness,"* who is he talking to, or about? Why does God use the plural words "us" and "our?"

At the core, we are all created in the image and likeness of God. This quotation does not refer to the creation of the physical body of man, but to the creation of the archetypal human, us at our innermost core, which is divine and immortal. Inside of each of us, in the innermost quiet space, housed within the soul, resides a spark of God.

I would like to share another beautiful sacred scripture that confirms this teaching.

> *When some of the Pharisees asked Jesus when the kingdom of God would come, he answered, saying to them, the kingdom of God does not come by observation. Neither will they say, Behold, it is here! or, behold, it is there! for behold, the kingdom of God is within you.* (Luke 17:20–21)

Similarly:

> *Do you not know that you are the temple of God, and the Spirit of God dwells in you?* (1 Corinthians 3:16)

It is this original creation of the archetypal man who is this "*Spirit of God* [who] *dwells in you*" and "*the kingdom of God is within you,*" that I will be calling the Universal Divine Child. It is the Universal Divine Child within each of us that you and I must be reawakened to. This is a part of our divine inheritance.

The Universal Divine Child

The Universal Divine Child is referred to in scripture by many different names, which can lead to confusion. To help avoid confusion, here is a list of some of the names used to describe the Universal Divine Child of God:

- Begotten Son of God,
- Son of God,

- Christ (Christian),
- Atman (Hindu),
- Self (with a capital "S"),
- Higher Self.

For now, when you think of these names, remember that they all mean the Universal Divine Child. In subsequent chapters, other than directly using the name Universal Divine Child, we will generally use only the name Higher Self.

The Universal Divine Child is one with God, but it has the appearance of being separated into all the souls that incarnate in an individual physical body. Our apparent separation from the Universal Divine Child is only an illusion.

The Universal Divine Child permeates the spiritual and material plains of existence as "higher consciousness." In this respect, when we use the term "higher consciousness," we mean the levels of consciousness at which we are aware of our unity and oneness with all of creation, both the material and the spiritual.

It is quite common for a spiritual being housed within a physical body to be conscious and aware of itself and the material world around it, but less aware, or even totally unaware, of the realities of "higher consciousness."

Higher consciousness, the essence of all spiritual beings, can be accessed while we are here on Earth. Spiritual masters past and present have learned to commune with higher consciousness—the Universal Divine Child—while living within the physical body.

Learning how to access higher consciousness is a path to the Kingdom of God and a component of your divine inheritance. This path, awareness, and ability to commune with higher consciousness is a birthright given freely to us by our Divine Parents. It is a great gift simply to know that this higher consciousness exists. This path to the Kingdom of God has been lost or forgotten for far too long.

People err by looking for God in some far off location. Actually God is closer to us than you may ever have imagined possible. If God wanted to hide from us (which I assure you, God does not), where would be the last place people would look for him? Answer: inside themselves.

When we adjust our perspectives from looking *outward* for the Kingdom of God to looking *inward* for our connection with God, we find ourselves pointed in the right direction. The Kingdom of God—reflected through the Universal Divine Child—is housed within each and every one of us.

The light of God, as reflected through the indwelling Universal Divine Child, is the light that illuminates every man and woman who comes into the world. This light exists whether people believe in God or not. This light exists in the hearts of black, white, brown, red, and yellow-skinned people. The outer skin color and culture may be different, but the inner connectivity with the Universal Divine Child and the Divine Parents is the same.

The Meaning of the Name Christ

The word "Christ" is derived from the Greek word *"Kristos,"* meaning "anointed." The Hebrew word for "Messiah" likewise means "anointed one." Essentially, an anointed person is one who has subdued (in other words, overcome and tamed) the Lower Attributes of the material world and fully lives in the divine connection and oneness with God. The christed person is a true reflection of, and operates his/her life in one accord with the Universal Divine Child. The anointed person's thoughts, words, and actions flow from living life in touch with Higher Attributes, which we shall discuss in chapters 17–23.

Anointing comes as a result of transmuting Lower Attribute vibrations in thoughts, words, and actions into Higher Attribute qualities—from living life in the physical world as a true reflection of the Universal Divine Child within. Anointing is a conscious process of discovering and consequently realizing unity with your true, divine, indwelling nature.

The word "Christ," therefore, should be viewed as a title and description of anyone transcending the personal ego of the Lower Self and merged with the Higher Self. The christed person has broken through the veil of darkness (ignorance) that the lower vibrations of the material world offer: the illusion that we are somehow separate from God. The christed person no longer lives in this state of illusion; he/she no longer believes he/she is separated from God. The christed person lives and breathes from a state of oneness with the Universal Divine Child who by and through its very nature is one with God.

Hereafter, this *state of awareness* of oneness with the Universal Divine Child, or Higher Self, will be referred to in this book as "Christ consciousness."

The christed person finds truth and lives in full awareness and realization of the statements *"I have said, You are gods; all of you are children of the most High,"* (Psalm 82:6) and *"Jesus said to them, Is it not so written in your law, I said, you are gods?"* (John 10:34)

Regardless of what tradition says, Christ is neither a first name, nor a last name of any single individual. Christ is a title for someone who is at one with the Universal Divine Child of God and, therefore, at one with God.

Jesuha ben Joseph, also known as Jesus of Nazareth, was anointed Christ by subduing the Lower Attribute characteristics of the material world and becoming one with the Universal Divine Child of God within himself, and therefore becoming one with God.

When the name Christ is used as Jesus's last name, we risk missing the point of many of this master's teachings. Many of his teachings were designed to show us that we are all sons and daughters of the living God. We could more accurately use the name "Jesus the Christ" or the "Christed Jesus" in describing Jeshua ben Joseph.

One of the greatest errors passed down through the years—one not based on original teachings—is the notion that because there is one God, there can only be one son of God. Master Jesus did not teach us that there is only *one* son of God. Nor did he claim that he was the *only* son of God. To the contrary, in John 20:17, it is written that Jesus said, *"I am ascending to my Father and your Father, and my God and your God."* This statement, among others, is not a statement someone would say if he held the belief that he was the "only" son of God.

We are all sons and daughters of God. We are all Divine Children.

Jesus the Christ, among others, is a clear demonstration for us all that the Universal Divine Child of God (the Higher Self) is real, alive, and resides within all men and women.

CHAPTER 3

Teachings of Jesus the Christ

"When the student is ready, the master appears."
—Buddhist Proverb

A S WE MOVE FORWARD with our remembrance of the Universal Divine Child of God, whom many call by the name Christ, we are now in a position to understand biblical scriptures with greater clarity. Our expanded perspective deepens our understanding of the teachings of Master Jesus.

We are told that Jesus was about thirty years old at the beginning of his public ministry. Prior to the time of his public ministry, we have record of the boy Jeshua ben Joseph who, at the age of twelve, traveled with this family to Jerusalem for the Passover feast, and was *"found in the temple, sitting in the midst of the teachers, listening to them and asking them questions."* (Luke 2:46)

It is quite interesting to find so little written about the early life of such a historically significant person as Jesus prior to his public ministry. The only events documented (in the Bible) in the next eighteen years or so—the missing years—is that *"Jesus grew in his stature and in his wisdom, and in favor with God and men."* (Luke 2:52). It is logical to assume that Jesus studied, learned, and taught during these missing eighteen years. As it relates to where he studied, what he studied, and with whom he studied, we will leave for another time as it is not the focus of this particular work.

At the beginning of Jesus' public ministry (John 1:9), John sets the stage for understanding the Universal Divine Child (the Higher Self within) and Christ consciousness. John testifies: *"He was the true light which lighted every man who came into the world."*

John states that a part of God resides in all people. We may call this part of God residing in all people a spark, a flame, or a light; the terms mean the same thing: that all souls incarnated into the world of matter have a part of God inside them as their birthright.

> *But those who received him* [become aware of the indwelling Universal Divine Child], *to them he gave power to become sons of God, especially to those who believed in his name* [the Christ]. (John 1:12)

Many people read this passage mentally interpreting the words "received him" and "in his name" to mean *Jesus the man*. Rather, it would appear that John meant to describe the Universal Divine Child of God. John makes this clear in the next verse.

> *And the Word became flesh and dwelt among us, and we saw his glory, a glory like that of the first born of the Father* [the Universal Divine Child], *full of grace and truth.* (John 1:14)

Here John compares the glory of the christed Jesus with the *"glory like that of the first born* [the Universal Divine Child] *of the Father* [and Mother]." Notice the "like that of" terminology used in the passage, this denotes a comparison.

John later writes:

> *This is the one of whom I said, He is coming after me, and*
> *yet he is ahead of me, because he was before me."* (John 1:15)

When John says, *"He is coming after me,"* he is describing the order of his and Jesus's public ministries. The Bible states that John preached, taught, and baptized before Jesus' public ministry. It appears that John was born before Jesus. So when John says, *"Yet he is ahead of me, because he was before me,"* John could not have meant "before me" in relation to their birth order. John is trying to provide insight that the one coming after him (Jesus) is more than just a man.

Jesus began his public ministry as a christed person, one who had become at-one with God by communing with the higher consciousness of the Universal Divine Child within him. Being aware of the higher consciousness of the Universal Divine Child (the Higher Self) within, is what we mean when we use the term "Christ consciousness."

Jesus Speaking from Two Perspectives

We can better understand Jesus's teachings by being aware that when he was teaching and speaking he spoke in two voices. That is, he taught from two different perspectives. He spoke from the perspective of Jesus the man *("I testify concerning myself")* and at other times he spoke from the perspective of the Universal Divine Child *("and my Father who sent me testifies concerning me")*.

> *And it is written in your own law that the testimony of two*
> *men is true. I testify concerning myself, and my Father who*
> *sent me testifies concerning me.* (John 8:17–18)

Similarly:

> *I do nothing of my own accord; but as my Father has taught me, so I speak just like him.* (John 8:28)

Once we identify the perspective used in a given passage, then we can better discern his message and use of the words "I," "me," "Christ," "Son of Man," and "Son of God." Learning to discern which perspective Jesus was teaching and testifying from will become more important as we learn more about the teachings about the Father, the Christ, and the Kingdom of God. In fact, we will see that many of Master Jesus's teachings make more sense once viewed from the correct perspective. Correctly understanding these teachings greatly assists us on our paths toward the seven victories of the Divine Child in our own lives.

Analyzing an example of Jesus speaking from two perspectives will clarify this point. Jesus said:

> *Your father Abraham rejoiced to see my day; and he saw it and was glad. The Jews said to him, "You are not yet fifty years old, and yet have you seen Abraham?" Jesus said to them, "Truly, truly, I say to you, Before Abraham was born, I was."* (John 8:56–58)

These two short verses are packed with information and spiritual insight. The phrase *"Abraham rejoiced to see my day,"* would appear to mean that Abraham was alive to observe and rejoice in Jesus's life and teachings on Earth. If the verse stopped there, we could say Jesus was just sharing his opinion on what Abraham's response might have been.

However, Jesus goes on to add, *"And he saw it and was glad."* Jesus did not say Abraham *sees* it and *is* glad, instead he says Abraham *saw* it and *was* glad—suggesting a time *before* the time in which he made this statement. Abraham died in approximately 1991 B.C., almost 2,000 years before Jesus made this statement. How could Jesus tell us that Abraham saw his day and was glad? This simple sentence conceals complex meanings. It could mean that Abraham, who was in spirit, could still watch and observe Jesus' day and was glad to see it. This, of course, would be true.

A deeper meaning is that *"my day"* refers to the time of the Universal Divine Child, a time long before Abraham was born into the world. Jesus meant that Abraham, while he was in spirit before he incarnated into the physical, saw the time of the Universal Divine Child and was glad.

It is quite clear that Jesus's audience did not understand what he was saying. They cited his age as proof that Jesus was not old enough to have known Abraham, let alone known if Abraham was glad.

It should be clear (referring to Jesus speaking from two perspectives), that Jesus could not have been speaking from a chronological perspective of himself as a man. However, his audience was trying to hear him from the perspective of Jesus the man talking and this is why they did not understand him. Hearing these two verses from the perspective of Jesus the man, *"not yet fifty years old,"* make no sense, thus the people wanted to stone him.

The next sentence of this same passage reveals a golden opportunity for those listening (both then and now) to understand that Jesus was speaking from the perspective of the Universal Divine Child within: *"Jesus said to them, Truly, truly, I say to you, Before Abraham was born, I was."* Jesus did not say he was born before Abraham. Jesus was trying to teach that before Abraham was born (or anyone for that matter), the Universal Divine Child existed.

This one example is illustrated to help us discern from which perspective Jesus was teaching from, from the perspective of himself (the son of Joseph) or from the perspective of the Universal Divine Child (son of God). You see, when a christed individual speaks—being one with the Universal Divine Child within— it is as if the Universal

Divine Child is the one speaking directly to the audience. Knowing this helps us to unlock many spiritual mysteries.

Higher Consciousness and Spiritual Wisdom

In John 4–6, Jesus was teaching about the "living water" and the "bread of life" to show that the Universal Divine Child is the higher consciousness and life force in our lives.

> *But whoever drinks of the water* [spiritual wisdom] *which I* [the Universal Divine Child] *give him shall never thirst; but the same water which I* [the Universal Divine Child] *give him shall become in him a well of water springing up to life everlasting.* (John 4:14)

In similar passages regarding the "bread of life," we read:

> *But my Father* [and your Father] *gives you the true bread from heaven. For the bread* [higher consciousness, life force] *of God is he* [the Universal Divine Child] *who has come down from heaven, who gives life to the world.* (John 6:32–33)

Parallel passages offer the same message:

> *I* [the Universal Divine Child] *am the bread of Life.* (John 6:35)

> *He who overcomes* [subdues the material world], *I* [the Universal Divine Child] *will give to eat of the hidden manna* [higher consciousness]. (Revelations 2:17)

> *Jesus also said: I have food to eat of which you do not know.* (John 4:32)

All these passages referring to *the living water* and *the bread of life* address higher consciousness of the Universal Divine Child that's available to all of God's children.

Consciousness, energy, or life force sustains all life from within; these are the spiritual living water and bread of life: the Universal Divine Child of God. God's life force enters the subtle body, then enters the physical body, like an electrical charge that causes our brains, nervous systems, and internal organs to function. Food and drink also provides energy. But it is God's life force, *his living water, his bread, and his hidden manna,* as reflected through the Universal Divine Child, that provides energy, consciousness, and life to our beings. Jesus wanted to be clear to all those listening that he wasn't talking about the bread and water of the physical world. He was referring to bread and water of the spiritual world.

It is written that he said:

> *It is the spirit* [of God through his Universal Divine Child] *that gives life; the body is of no account, the worlds which I have spoken to you are spirit and life.* (John 6:63)

Here again, those listening to Jesus did not appear to understand his teachings about God's Universal Divine Child, higher consciousness, and life force. When Jesus used the first person pronoun "I," they heard and interpreted the word to mean the human man instead of hearing him from the point of view of someone who has merged with the Universal Divine Child within himself. Once again, when a christed individual speaks—being one with the Universal Divine Child within—it is as if the Universal Divine Child is the one speaking directly to the audience.

> *This is the bread* [higher consciousness, life force] *which came down from heaven* [from the spiritual into the material world], *that a man may eat of it* [be nourished

33

in spiritual wisdom] *and not die* [the soul and spirit live on after the physical body dies]. *I* [the Universal Divine Child] *am the living bread* [higher consciousness] *because I came down from heaven* [and dwell within you]; *if any man eats of this bread, he shall live forever; and the bread* [higher consciousness, life force] *which I* [the Universal Divine Child] *am giving for the sake of the life of the world.* (John 6:50–51)

These passages disclose Master Jesus's attempts to inform his listeners about higher consciousness, spiritual wisdom, and life force from a higher plane of vibration: from Spirit. This energy is stepped down in intensity from God through the Universal Divine Child to all living beings. When we understand and acknowledge that the Spirit of God provides our individual souls and physical bodies with life, and that life and spirit are everlasting, we begin to approach the concept of Christ consciousness. We make the way straight for an increased amount of light and higher consciousness to enter our beings.

Whoever believes in me [speaking from the perspective of the Universal Divine Child within—not the man Jesus], *just as the scriptures have said, the rivers of living water* [spiritual wisdom flowing from the higher consciousness] *shall flow from within him.* (John 7:38)

When we understand and believe in the Universal Divine Child (the Higher Self that pervades all creation) we can *will* and *consciously intend* God's universal energy of light and life to increase its flow in us, and through us to others.

Later in the book we'll discuss how to make ourselves more open to higher consciousness on our path to the seven victories of the Divine Child.

I [the Universal Divine Child of God] *am the light* [life force] *of the world; he who follows me* [seeks higher consciousness and discovers the Universal Divine Child within himself/herself] *shall not walk in darkness* [ignorance that resides in the material illusions of the world and lack of spiritual knowledge], *but shall find for himself the light of life.* (John 8:12)

The Higher Self—the Universal Divine Child— perceived through raising our consciousness is available for all of us to discover for ourselves. The Higher Self will lead us to, and through the Higher Attributes while we live in this material world. Once we allow the Higher Self to lead us and we begin living the Higher Attributes, we become clearer reflections of who we really are: sons and daughters of God.

The Doorway to the Kingdom

Far too many people seek the doorway to the Kingdom of God outside of themselves, as if the doorway were somewhere "out there." Too often they believe they can pass through the doorway to the Kingdom of God only *after* physical death. Neither of these outdated or misunderstood perspectives comport with what the spiritual masters from many traditions have taught us.

The doorway to the Kingdom of God is found within. It is an internal, not an external doorway. The stepping stones that lead to the doorway are *will* and *intention*. The doorway can be opened, and we may consciously "come in and go out" of the Kingdom of God while still being alive in the physical world.

The first step in reaching this doorway is to change our perspective and realize:

1. There is a doorway on the path, and
2. The doorway on the path can be found within.

Christ consciousnesses, the state of awareness of our oneness with God, is the path to the Kingdom of God. It is the doorway leading to the victories of the Divine Child. Biblical scripture references the doorway in these terms:

> *I* [the Higher Self within all men and women] *am the way and the truth and the life; no man comes to my Father* [and your Father] *except by me* [the Higher Self]. (John 14:6)

Also:

> *To him the doorkeeper* [the Higher Self within] *opens the door* [to higher consciousness] *and the sheep hear his voice, and he calls his own sheep by their names and brings them out.* (John 10:3)

And in a parallel passage:

> *I* [the Higher Self within] *am the door; if any man enter by me* [through higher consciousness], *he shall live and he shall come in and go out and find pasture.* (John 10:9)

These references to the door and the doorkeeper offer several levels of meaning. The first level is the plain meaning of the words chosen. The next level reflects what is understood by those who have ears to hear Jesus's true message. The final level of meaning is a call to hear the voice within our souls, calling out for us to reunite in oneness with God. The still small voice of the Higher Self is available to all those who have prepared themselves to perceive it. We might ask what *"if any man enter by me"* means. Enter what? Enter where? It means to enter into the secret, silent, space-less space of the omnipotent God through the Higher Self within. *"He shall come in and go out and find pasture"* means man shall enter into the Kingdom of God and alternate between the material world in consciousness and the Kingdom of God in Christ consciousness, and find peace, love, and nourishment for the soul.

> *His disciples said to him, When will the Kingdom come? (Jesus said), It will not come by waiting for it. It will not be a matter of saying, "here it is," or "there it is," Rather, the kingdom of the father is spread out upon the earth, and men do not see it. (The Gospel of Thomas,* saying 113)

Perhaps one of the reasons we do not see the Kingdom of God spread out upon the Earth is because we are seeking a doorway outside of ourselves. If we look for a doorway in the wrong place, we will not find it. When we look for the doorway in the right place, the doorway becomes apparent to us.

The Father and Son

In John 10:30, it is written:

> *I* [Jesus] *and my Father* [the Universal Divine Child presence within me] *are of one accord.*

This affirms that the Universal Divine Child of God is the Higher Self, and that The Universal Divine Child is also our spiritual Father. Moreover, the Universal Divine Child resides within all men and women.

Please note that gender at the level of spirit is androgynous, neither male nor female, but energetically has aspects of both genders. In the *Illustrated Book of Sacred Scriptures* (Quest Books, 1998), Timothy Freke discusses the fact that through translations we often lose some of the power behind the meaning of certain terms. For example, he says, *"Jesus called God Abwoon, an Aramaic term normally translated* as '*father.' But it could equally well be rendered in a gender-neutral way as 'parent' or 'mother-father' or even 'the breath of life that comes from the All.'"*

Because this concept may be different from what you were once taught, you may find it helpful to use the family tree as an analogy. To clarify these teachings of the Father and son, let us utilize the ancient Hermetic axiom "As above, so below; as below, so above."

Physical Example

You have an earthly father.

Your earthly father in turn has a father (your grandfather).

Your earthly father is thus the son of his father (your grandfather).

So, your earthly father is *both* a father and a son.

Spiritual Example

We have a spiritual father (the Universal Divine Child).

Our spiritual father (the Universal Divine Child) in turn has a spiritual father/mother (God).

Our spiritual father (the Universal Divine Child) is the begotten child of the father/mother God.

Therefore, our spiritual father (the Universal Divine Child) is *both* a father and a child.

Our Father, the Universal Divine Child, is often called "the Christ." Remember, it's as Jesus the Christ said in John 5:43, "*I have come in the name of my Father.*"

Another important passage in the Bible that relates to the Father and Child relationship is:

> *Call no one on earth, Father, for one is your Father in heaven. Nor be called leaders, for one is your leader, the Christ.* (Matthew 23:9–10)

The spiritual terminology of father and son that many Christians grew up with (or perhaps just have grown accustomed to), can prevent us from seeing clearly the relationships in the family tree set forth above.

An additional passage, taken from the less-often quoted *The Gospel of Truth*, found in the *The Nag Hammadi Library*, confirms these relationships:

> *Now, the end is receiving knowledge about the one who is hidden, and this is the Father, from whom the beginning came forth, to whom all will return who have come forth from him. Now the name of the Father is the Son. It is he who first gave a name to the one who came forth from him, who was himself, and he begot him as a son. He gave him his name which belonged to him; he is the one to whom belongs all that exists around him, the Father. His is the name; his is the Son. It is possible for him to be seen. The name, however, is invisible because it alone is the mystery of the invisible which comes to ears that are completely filled with it by him. For indeed, the Father's name is not spoken, but it is apparent through a Son. It is the Father. The Son is his name.*

Master Jesus acknowledged, believed, and based his every move upon the fact that he was one with the Universal Divine Child within himself. He had Christ consciousness. He taught us by example that we, too, can move into a state of higher consciousness and be at one with the Universal Divine Child within us.

In John 14:6, Master Jesus said he is the way to his father. It is unfortunate that this passage has been misinterpreted for so many years. The error stems from the assumption that Jesus, the man, was talking, rather than the Universal Divine Child within him. For centuries, people have interpreted this passage literally. Unfortunately, a literal reading distracts us from Jesus's actual teachings about our spiritual father, whose presence abides in all men and women.

John 14:6 can be interpreted in a more spiritual way that points out the path to the Kingdom of God:

> *Jesus said to him* [Thomas], *I* [the Universal Divine Child of God within me and within you] *am the way* [the doorway to the Kingdom of God] *and the truth* [that your soul is longing for] *and the life* [God's light that gives and sustains the life of all things material and spiritual]; *no man comes to my Father* [and your Father] *except by me* [the Universal Divine Child].

Later in the same chapter, Philip asks Jesus directly about his Father. Jesus responds that the father resided within him, again alluding to the fact that he was speaking from two perspectives. Jesus explains that he is not speaking for himself as a human man, but as a representative of the Universal Divine Child within him, when he claims to be the way to the Father.

> *The words that I speak unto you I speak not of myself: but the Father that dwelleth in me.* (John 14:10, *King James Bible*)

Jesus did not want to lead people to worship him. That wasn't the purpose of claiming to be the way to the Father. In fact, it would have been contrary to the core of his message about God. Instead, Master Jesus wanted to lead people to:

- A fresh understanding of a loving, forgiving God.
- Awareness that we are all children of God, with a part of God dwelling within us.
- Love (not fear) God with our hearts, souls, and minds, and to love our neighbors (our fellow spiritual brothers and sisters) as ourselves.

His Promise and Our Inheritance

Master Jesus, with his Christ consciousness, bequeathed us a valuable inheritance when he said:

> *Truly, truly, I say to you, He who believes in me* [the Universal Divine Child of God who dwells within] *shall do the works which I* [Jesus] *do; and even greater than these things shall he do because I am going to my Father.* (John 14:12)

How often do we hear this passage quoted? Why is it that we seldom hear about this great promise and inheritance? Master Jesus told us directly that when we really believe and understand that the Universal Divine Child of God dwells within us, and seek the Kingdom of God by becoming one with the Universal Divine Child, we shall do the works that Jesus did, and even greater works.

We must stop believing in God in such a way that causes us to feel we are unworthy of inheriting this promise. My friend, never let *anyone* tell you or make you feel that you are not worthy. You are made in the image and likeness of God. You have the spirit of God dwelling within you! This alone makes you worthy of Jesus's bequest and promise.

We must strive to live our lives consistent with the examples that Master Jesus and other spiritual masters have shown us. We must strive to live our lives consistent with the Higher Attributes you'll soon learn about. Every single person has the opportunity to experience and, in turn, know firsthand, the peace and outpouring of God's love into their very being. Every single person has the opportunity to experience the victories of the Divine Child and seek the Kingdom of God *while still alive on Earth.*

To live the promise, and accept the inheritance, we must awaken each day with the conscious intention to increase our awareness of the Universal Divine Child's presence inside us. Awareness of the

Higher Self will generate an expansion of our consciousness, up to and including being at one with the Higher Self within. Consciousness of the presence of the Higher Self is a gift that God has freely given us. Living each day in alignment with the Higher Attributes causes God's light within us to shine brighter and brighter. God's unmanifested presence, through the light within, becomes manifested in our lives through our thoughts, words, and actions.

> *Do you not know that you are the temple of God, and that the Spirit of God dwells in you?* (1 Corinthians 3:16)

CHAPTER 4

Where Is the Kingdom of God?

"The kingdom of God does not come by observation.
Neither will they say, Behold, it is here! Or, behold, it is
there! For behold, the kingdom of God is within you."
—The Gospel of Luke (17:20–21)

M ANY OF THE TEACHINGS regarding the Kingdom of God have been taught in parables, or stories, that contain layers of hidden meaning. Not unlike peeling back the layers of an onion to reach its core, oftentimes we must peel back the layers of a parable to reach its core meaning. It appears that when Master Jesus taught about the Kingdom of God, as recorded in the New Testament of the Christian Bible, many of the people hearing his message didn't understand the parables.

Instead of attempting a full dissection of the many parables regarding the Kingdom of God, we'll place our attention now on several more overt passages written in the New Testament, the non-canonical Gospels (those not embraced by the Catholic Church and other sects), and other spiritual writings. The first of these is Matthew 6:33:

Seek first the kingdom of God and his righteousness, and all these things shall be added to you.

To this day, if one hundred randomly selected people were asked the question, "Where is the Kingdom of God?" what do you suppose would be the majority's answer? I submit, the majority would answer, "Heaven," and heaven would be described as a location *"out there someplace."* They might even point up at the sky.

For many, it is believed that the Kingdom of God can only be experienced after physical death. However, as you either know now or will come to realize, the Kingdom of God can be experienced while you are alive in the physical body. As stated in The Lord's Prayer:

Thy kingdom come, thy will be done, as in heaven so on earth. (Matthew 6:10)

Seeking the Kingdom of God is to seek sacred unity with God right here and right now. Seeking the kingdom is to seek a state of conscious awareness of oneness with God, and to know that we have never been separated from God, for all life is in God. God is life, and this includes life beyond our experience of inhabiting a physical body.

To enter a conscious awareness of the Kingdom of God, we read where we can be born again and become like little children. In John (3:3), we see the first reference Jesus made regarding the Kingdom of God. Jesus tells Nicodemus, *"Truly, truly, I say to you, If a man is not born again, he cannot see the kingdom of God."*

Many attempts at interpreting *"born again"* have made their way into religious traditions. What does it mean to be born again? We have to take a step back into Jesus's native language to understand this saying. A footnote in George Lamsa's translation of the Bible from the original Aramaic explains, *"Born again in northern Aramaic means: 'to change one's thoughts and habits' Nicodemus spoke southern Aramaic and hence did not understand Jesus."*

When we change our thoughts and habits from thinking about the Divine Presence *out there someplace*, into thoughts and habits of being united with God here and now, our entire perspective changes. Our perceptions of God, life, and our oneness with God change in a way that causes us to see everything anew. These changes are so significant that we feel we have born again, and we have a renewed perspective of God and of his divine presence in our lives. We feel as if we have been born again with a renewed sense of closeness and understanding, gained through our enlightened state of consciousness. It is difficult to put this new state of consciousness into words, so it is simply stated as, "We have been born again."

Jesus said:

> *Truly I say to you, Unless you change and become like little children, you shall not enter into the kingdom of heaven.* (Matthew 18:3)

To help understand the meaning of this passage, think about the attributes of a child. Children are fearless. They have no guilt (unless they have been taught it). They are loving, honest, and live in the present moment. Children *believe first* and therefore can see the wonders of life. Unlike most adults, who need to *see first* and *then* they will believe. Reclaiming the attributes of a child, while being born anew in our conscious oneness with God leads us victoriously onwards on the path to the Kingdom of God and claiming our divine inheritance.

The Kingdom of God Inside and Outside of Us

Let us look at another passage taken from *The Gospel of Thomas*. Here Jesus is reported to have said:

> *If those who lead you say to you, "See, the kingdom is in the sky," then the birds of the sky will precede you. If they*

say to you, "It is in the sea, then the fish will precede you."
Rather, the kingdom is inside of you, and it is outside of you.
When you come to know yourselves, then you will become
known, and you will realize that it is you who are the sons
of the living father. (Saying 3)

In this passage Jesus directs our attention to *where* we can look for (and find) the Kingdom of God. We are told that the kingdom is *both* inside and outside of us; or in other words, everywhere. This saying makes total sense in light of the belief that God is the unity of all life and that we live, move, and experience our being inside of God.

Asked, "Where would God's kingdom *not* be?" we could answer: Nowhere. God's kingdom would not, could not, be outside of God's presence. God is omnipresent.

The disciples also asked Jesus, *"When* will the Kingdom of God come?" This, too, sounds like an honest, inquisitive question. In fact, many people are still asking the same question today! The question of *when* the Kingdom will come is filled with the presupposition that there is, or was, a period of time in which it did not exist.

Jesus was basically saying, "Listen people, your awareness and realization of the Kingdom of God won't come by you just waiting for it. The kingdom is not going to just show up one day and you'll say, 'Oh, look, there it is over there.' No, the Kingdom of God is here and around you; you just don't recognize it yet."

Wow! Does the last sentence in this passage come as a surprise to you? Whenever I have shared this concept with people, I receive open-mouthed, wide-eyed stares. Within a few minutes, someone will ask, "Well, *if* the Kingdom of God *is* spread out upon the Earth, *how* can we learn to see (perceive) it?" Perhaps another question that would be useful for us to ask ourselves is, "How do my perceptions need to change for me to be aware of my sacred unity with God and his kingdom?"

Jesus described the Kingdom of God as being so close to us (closer than the nose on our faces) that we often don't see it. We don't perceive God's kingdom because our perspective, which is influenced by our perception, is looking elsewhere for the presence of God. Where God's presence is, you will find his kingdom.

Considering the same question of where the Kingdom of God is, but looking at it through the lens of a different set of spiritual writings, let us consider a passage from *The Aquarian Gospel of Jesus the Christ* by Levi (DeVorss & Company, 1907). In this passage, Ajainin, a priest, asks Jesus about the kingdom of the "Holy One." Ajainin asks, "Where is the kingdom? Where is the king?"

> *And Jesus said, This kingdom is not far away, but man with mortal eyes can see it not; it is within the heart. You need not seek the king in earth, or sea, or sky; he is not there, and yet is everywhere. He is the Christ* [the Universal Divine Child] *of God; is universal love.* (29:19–20)

There is a correlation between the passage we have just reviewed, *"But man with mortal eyes can see it not"* and the Saying 113 from *The Gospel of Thomas: "The kingdom of the father is spread out upon the earth, and men do not see it."* In both, Jesus touches on the limitations of our physical senses, specifically, the limitation of our sense of sight.

We have become overly reliant on what our five senses report to us. We mistakenly interpret the limited vibrational wavelength that our physical eyes can perceive as reality. When we open ourselves up and expand our perceptions beyond what our physical senses report to us, we can move forward in our perception of God and the kingdom.

Whereas the last several passages we looked at focused on *both* the Kingdom of God inside and outside of us, the next few will focus only on the aspect of the Kingdom of God inside us. Although you'll see many similarities to the passages already highlighted, there is value in focusing our attention on those that relate to the kingdom within.

In the New Testament of the Bible, written in *The Gospel of Luke*, some of the Pharisees were questioning Master Jesus regarding the Kingdom of God and again asking *when* the Kingdom will come. Jesus answered, saying to them:

> *The kingdom of God does not come by observation. Neither will they say, Behold, it is here! or, behold, it is there! for behold, the kingdom of God is within you.* (Luke 17:20–21)

This is such a powerful and meaningful message! In this passage Jesus doesn't talk to us in a parable, he is clear and to the point: "*The kingdom of God is within you.*"

I ask (largely to the reader of the Christian tradition), how often have you heard this passage from Master Jesus preached in church? It is my observation only (certainly not a judgment), that the answer is rarely, if ever, taught in church. If this is your observation as well, why is it that we do not hear more about this significant message?

Either way, taught or not taught, we now know, or at least we have it in our consciousness, that the Kingdom of God is inside of us.

In *The Gospel of Thomas*, saying 109, we read:

> *Jesus said, the kingdom is like a man who had a hidden treasure in his field without knowing it.*

In a similar passage found in *The Gospel of Matthew* (13:44), we read:

> *The kingdom of heaven is like a treasure which is hidden in the field, which a man discovered and hid, and because of his joy, he went and sold everything he had, and bought that field.*

We know that many of the people Jesus taught in his travels were farmers. Jesus spoke to them in terms that they could relate to in their everyday life, terms like seeds, sowing, fields, and so on. But when is a field not a tract of land?

The Hindu scripture of *The Bhagavad Gita* describes the field and the knower of the field. In chapter 13, verse 1, we read, *"The body is called a field."*

In *The Gospel of Thomas,* saying 109, we read that the kingdom is like a hidden treasure in a man's field, but he does not know it (meaning, he isn't aware of the treasure). The treasure is hidden in the field: the body.

What is the "hidden treasure" in the body of a man that he is unaware of? The hidden treasure is the presence of the Divine, the reflection of Spirit within man. As stated in quote from Matthew, when a man discovers what is hidden in the field of his body, he is joyful to the extent that other possessions in his material life pale in comparison.

As we put these pieces of spiritual writings together to help us form a clear picture, lastly we read:

> *And Jesus said, I cannot show the king, unless you see with eyes of soul, because the kingdom of the king is in the soul. And every soul a kingdom is. There is a king for every man. This king is love, and when this love becomes the greatest power in life, it is the Christ* [the Universal Divine Child/ the Higher Self]; *so Christ is king. And every one may have this Christ dwell in his soul, as Christ dwells in my soul.* (The Aquarian Gospel of Jesus the Christ 71:4–7)

We can integrate the learning's from the teachings of Jesus the Christ, and the teachings of *The Bhagavad Gita* into the last passage of this section.

Once again, we read that we cannot see the Kingdom of God within a person with our physical eyes, but we can perceive it with the "eyes of the soul." Every man and woman, regardless of age, race, color, or religious belief, has, as his or her birthright, the kingdom of the soul within him or her. This kingdom is love.

Later on, we will talk about our Higher Attributes, all of which flow out of love. When our Lower Attributes are transmuted into Higher Attributes, the Christ, the Higher Self, reins in our thoughts, our words, and our actions.

Truly, the Kingdom of God is at hand!

PART TWO

Allow God to Guide You Each Step of the Way

*"There are two kinds of people: those
who say to God, 'Thy will be done,'
and those to whom God says,
'All right, then, have it your way.'"*

—C.S. Lewis

CHAPTER 5
The Higher Self

"The Truth is One and the learned
call it by many names."
—Rig Veda

THE TOPIC OF THE HIGHER SELF may be one of the more complicated to describe and to understand. One of the challenges of describing the Higher Self stems from the fact that it has been referred to by so many different names in the past. The Higher Self is not a new spiritual concept. Quite the contrary. References to the characteristics and workings have been taught directly and indirectly by many traditions throughout history in their sacred scriptures.

We have arrived in our present-day world with a fragmented, patchwork exposure to higher truths. Our current age is a fertile ground for these seeds of truth to grow into clearer understanding. Perhaps now we are more open to exploring the parts and pieces of truth that have found their way into the puzzle. The truth is beginning to take shape as something we can recognize. You can come to recognize the Higher Self. It is truly a gift from God and, as you will see, it is far closer to each of us than you may have ever imagined.

Bright but hidden, the Self dwells in the heart. Everything that moves, breathes, opens, and closes lives in the Self. He is the source of love and may be known through love but not through thought. He is the goal of life. Attain this goal! The shining Self dwells hidden in the heart. Everything in the cosmos, great and small, lives in the Self. He is the source of life, truth beyond the transience of this world. He is the goal of life. Attain this goal! (Mundaka Upanishad 2.2:1–2)

The Higher Self, which is synonymous with the Universal Divine Child of God as we saw in Part One, is one with God and acts as a divine reflection of God within the hearts and minds of men and women. It has long been a mystery how the Higher Self, while never separating connection with God, can manifest into the *apparently* separate identities of people incarnated in the material world. Due to our *apparently* separate identities, it is easy to conclude that each of us has our own Higher Self. In truth, there is but one Higher Self manifesting through all people.

The individual self, or the ego self (which I shall term the *Lower Self* to draw a distinction), is, in fact, unique to an individual's personal experience. Nonetheless, every person maintains the universal core characteristics, functions, and purpose of the Higher Self. How these common core characteristics show up and can be observed in the individual person's thoughts, words, and actions varies widely from person to person.

The Higher Self is the link connecting the individual, incarnated person and the Divine. In this moment, it does not matter if we are consciously aware of it; some people are, some people aren't. In either case, it exists. It would be a true statement, however, to say that conscious awareness of the indwelling divinity in us strengthens our connection to the Divine, leading us to *"at-onement"* with the Higher Self (through Christ consciousness), and, as a natural extension, at-onement with the Divine Father/Mother.

The Higher Self

Historically, people have had misperceptions about where to place their awareness, energy, and focus in order to form a connection with the Divine. In old religious paradigms, awareness and attention was placed on looking upward and outward to the sky, to the place where people believed *heaven*, a residence for God, was. All along, connection with God, through the Higher Self, could be found within.

That God is found within makes sense when you consider the Higher Attribute of love. Does love originate from outside of us? Or does love flow outward from within?

For far too long, far too many people have been taught, and have accepted, the erroneous notion that they're not worthy to have the divine connection so close to them, closer than the nose on their face. The thought processes related to looking upward and outward seeking oneness with God has done nothing more than perpetuate the consciousness of separation from God.

Our purpose in life is to bring Higher Attributes into our daily experiences through our direct connection with God within us—through the Higher Self: *"Father, let thy will be done in the earthly plane as it is in the spiritual plane."* We are all well equipped and capable of manifesting our true divine nature on a daily basis.

It is true to say that we have all manifested some form of divinity into our daily lives, though some people perhaps more than others. What we are discussing here is to discover how, through *at-onement* with the Higher Self, we may manifest divinity into our lives consciously and with greater regularity.

At-onement with God is not an action or a process reserved for a select few of us to experience while incarnated in a material body; it is a birthright for every member of humanity. In truth, race, gender, color, creed, and religion play no role in this way of being. All of us are children of God. All are sons and daughters of God. For what is the race of the soul? What is the color of the soul? What is the earthly religion of the soul?

Human beings are 99 percent the same. Yet some of us choose to spend time, energy and emotion focusing on the 1 percent that is different. The world would be a better place to live if instead we were to celebrate the differences and embrace our unity, for we are all spiritual beings having a human experience together. At the level of spirit, these differences are just an illusion.

When we honestly and sincerely say in our minds, "Not my will God, but let thy will be done," and feel the meaning of this statement in our hearts, we are in essence surrendering our human will and inviting God's presence, intelligence, and will into our being. By virtue of inviting God's will into our lives—here and now—we are stating an intention for the Universal Divine Child of God, to move forward from the back seat into the driver's seat of our lives.

Especially for those involved in a crisis, the act of surrendering can happen in an instant. A crisis often acts as a catalyst in breaking down our ego defenses. For others, surrendering to God's will is a step-by-step process. Either way requires of us a measure of faith. Either way requires a measure of trust. That is, until faith and trust are no longer needed because you just *know*.

Who and What Is the Higher Self?

The Higher Self is the archetype (original pattern or model) on which humanity was created. The Higher Self (the Universal Divine Child) is the eternally begotten, primordial child created by its divine parents, our Father/Mother God.

One of the most wondrous mysteries of creation is how the abiding Universal Divine Child of God, a divine reflection of the Father/Mother, *is one with all life and dwells within all people.*

Many wisdom traditions point their teachings in the same direction using different terminology. Because of this, on the surface, it appears that these traditions are talking about different things. They are not. A closer look reveals unity, not differences. I would like to share some beautiful, thought-provoking wisdom from the Hindu tradition with you now that clearly illustrates the nature of the Higher Self.

The teachings of Sri Krishna appear in the Hindu scripture *The Bhagavad Gita* (from Sanskrit, meaning, *The Song of the Lord*). Krishna is an incarnation, one of several avatars, of the God Vishnu. Vishnu (the maintainer/preserver) is one of a Hindu Trinity that also includes Shiva (the destroyer/transformer) and Brahma (the creator). Historians place the events depicted in *The Bhagavad Gita,* scenes of epic battles and warfare, somewhere between 1000 and 700 B.C. Hindus believe that Vishnu incarnates on Earth from time to time, age after age, in order to rekindle divine law and vanquish the powers of darkness.

In his Introduction to his translation of *The Bhagavad Gita,* Eknath Easwaran writes, "*The Gita's* subject is the war within, the struggle for self-mastery that every human being must wage if he or she is to emerge from life victorious. ... Krishna is not some external being, human or superhuman, but the spark of divinity that lies at the core of the human personality."

Consider these lines from the text:

> *It* [God as the Higher Self] *dwells in all, in every hand and foot and head, in every mouth and eye and ear in the universe. ... Completely independent, it supports all things. ... It is both near and far, both within and without every creature; it moves and is unmoving. In its subtlety it is beyond comprehension. It is indivisible, yet appears divided in separate creatures. Dwelling in every heart, it is beyond darkness. It is called the light of lights.* (The Bhagavad Gita 13:13–17)

The *Atman* is also called the Self, the Higher Self or the Divine Self by the Hindus. The Atman is one with Brahman, the impersonal Godhead. All deities in the Hindu tradition are different aspects, but are describing one supreme God (Brahman). The Higher Self is none other than God's presence in all human beings. It is not separated from God. Nor is the Higher Self separated from any one of us. The Higher Self is one with God. The Lower Self, or self written with a lowercase "S," denotes the individual human personality, or ego self, which thinks of itself as being separate from God. Understanding the teachings of the Higher Self, the divinity within all creation, leads us in our further understanding of the Universal Divine Child within.

Krishna encourages us to allow Atman (the Higher Self) to guide us:

> *The senses are higher than the body, the mind higher than the senses; above the mind is the intellect, and above the intellect is the Atman. Thus, knowing that which is supreme, let the Atman rule the ego.* (The Bhagavad Gita 3:42–43)

Krishna teaches us to allow the Higher Self (the Atman) to rule the Lower Self. In other words, Krishna taught us to make the choice to *allow* our true Self—the Higher Self within—to rule over the impermanent ego self. It is important to point out that intending and allowing this change to take place within us is a conscious choice.

Now that we know we have a choice, we can consciously choose to make moment-by-moment decisions that allow us to be led by the Higher Self.

When we choose to make the change from being led by the ego self to being led by the Higher Self, we are born again. In this context, "born again" means that we've changed our thoughts and habits from those that support or reinforce the ego, to those that flow naturally out of the Higher Self. For most of us, this is a process of self-transformation. Among other things, it is the expansion of our consciousness that allows us to see the Divine within all people.

> *My true being is unborn and changeless. I am the Lord who dwells in every creature.* (The Bhagavad Gita 4:6)

I am ever present to those who have realized me in every creature. Seeing all life as my manifestation, they are never separated from me. They worship me in the hearts of all, and all their actions proceed from me. Wherever they may live, they abide in me. (The Bhagavad Gita 6:30–31)

When (not *if*), in our spiritual maturity, we become aware enough to perceive the Higher Self in every person, the characteristics of the ego self and the Lower Attributes that have given the ego self its sense of identity, begin to dissolve.

I look upon all creatures equally; none are less dear to me and none more dear. But those who worship me [keep me in their thoughts, seek me] *with love live in me, and I come to life in them.* (The Bhagavad Gita 9:29)

I liken the last part of this verse, *"I come to life in them,"* to the analogy of the Divine Ember. The Divine Ember (a spark or flame symbolic of the Higher Self) is housed within. Much like blowing air on a softly glowing ember in a fireplace, when a person consciously acknowledges the Higher Self within, it's as if God breathes a holy breath on this indwelling ember, causing its glow to brighten. Additionally, when we align our thoughts, words and actions with the Higher Attributes (which we'll discuss in greater detail in a later chapter), God once again breathes upon the indwelling ember, causing its light to radiate throughout our being *("I come to life in them")*.

When our conscious choices become clearer reflections of the Higher Self within us, the outside world becomes more like the inside world and the two become as one. This is the pathway to the victory of the Divine Child. This means you!

This supreme Self [the Higher Self] *is without beginning, undifferentiated, deathless. Though it dwells in the body,*

Arjuna, it neither acts nor is touched by action. As akasha pervades the cosmos but remains unstained, the Self can never be tainted though it dwells in every creature. (The Bhagavad Gita 13:31–32)

In this passage, Sri Krishna describes the supreme Self as unaffected by the actions and dramas in life. He said the Higher Self is above the law of cause and effect and the law of karma. In other words, who we really are in our divinity, stands above our lives and remains untouched and unaffected by the hurts, pains, and troubles of living in a dualistic world. For now, when I say dualistic world, it means a world in which opposites exist.

Within the body the supreme Purusha [the Higher Self within], *is called the witness, approver, supporter, enjoyer, the supreme Lord, the higher Self. Some realize the Self within them through the practice of meditation, some by the path of wisdom, and others by selfless service.* (The Bhagavad Gita 12:22–24)

Although Sri Krishna goes into much more detail in *The Bhagavad Gita* about the paths of meditation (Raja Yoga), knowledge (Jnana Yoga), wisdom and devotion (Bhakti Yoga), and selfless service (Karma Yoga), he also tells us that all paths lead to God.

As men approach me, so I receive them. All paths, Arjuna, lead to me. (The Bhagavad Gita 4:11)

Preceding taking any path, it is helpful to be reminded of the actual goal: rediscovering our oneness with God. Here is Krishna's reminder to us:

I [the God inside and outside of you] *am the goal of life* [to realize your oneness with me]; *the Lord and support of all, the inner witness, the abode of all. I am the only refuge, the one true friend.* (The Bhagavad Gita 9:18)

Oneness with God, the ultimate experience in life, is the destination our souls long for, and it is our divine inheritance. In fact, our souls have been leading us to rediscovery of God all along. We lose sight of this destination at times because our lives push and pull us in many different directions. We get so caught up in playing the role of being human that we forget the purpose of the play. Our minds run constantly, anxious and restless, oftentimes drowning out the still small voice within, and not heeding its guidance. We frequently shrug off the voice in our hearts—called *intuition*—discounting it as our imagination, and then we go back to playing our individual roles.

When we hear and reflect on the words of a spiritual master, such as Jesus or Krishna, which come to us through God-inspired scriptures, such as *The Holy Bible, The Upanishads,* and *The Bhagavad Gita,* we put on the brakes. We stop acting for a short time and we are reminded of the main point of the play.

We are invited, through gaining an expanded perspective, to move beyond the limited confines of believing "I am my body," and into the awareness of "I am one with the Higher Self, the Divine within me." It is through our growing awareness of the Higher Self that we can claim and experience our divine inheritance, our oneness with God.

Many folks think that they have to experience their physical death in order to realize God. I am here to say—as others have said before—that we can experience the Higher Self, the Atman, the Universal Divine Child within, while we are here on the Earth in the physical body. This is the path to the Kingdom of God. This is the destination our souls long for.

Sometimes we may have to *unlearn* that which we have learned in order to make room for new lessons. Whatever we believe now requires faith. And faith is a wonderful thing. Faith is a power that can lead us to further understanding. Faith, however, is not an end point. It is an evolution, a process. On the other side of faith is knowing. If we think about it, we can see that faith is no longer needed once we come to the place where "we know that we know."

Nothing and no one is separate from God. God is all that there is. Seek to know God. Seek to know the Higher Self within. Seek to see the Divine Child in every face. All of these expressions convey the same idea. This is your path to claim your divine inheritance.

For many reasons, people can find it difficult to believe in the Higher Self. By extension, they find it difficult to accept the statement that "a part of God dwells within all people." Please be aware of how you feel inside, at the core of your being, when you reflect upon this statement and these ideas. I ask you only to be aware, not to judge, how you feel about them. Is there a level of resistance? Is there a level of acceptance? Is there some feeling of both resistance and acceptance? Either way is okay, just be aware of what your internal dialogue is saying.

In further describing the Higher Self, when we read about the "Father" in the Bible it can be helpful to think about the Father as the Higher Self. As Master Jesus taught in *The Gospel of Matthew* (23:9–10):

> *And call no one on earth, Father, for one is your Father in heaven. Nor be called leader, for one is your leader, the Christ.*

What was Jesus teaching us in this passage? First, he is telling us that we have one Father, the creator of the real you—the individualized soul—housed within God. Also, Jesus is teaching us that the Christ (the Higher Self) is our leader and will lead us through life, guiding us every step along the way. Of course, this happens only if we surrender to God's will and allow this leadership into our life. Through our own free will, we can do so, or we can choose to struggle through life on our own led only by the ego self. As with most things, this, too, is a choice.

Later on, in Part Five, "The Battles and Victories of the Divine Child," we'll explore how the Higher Self (when acknowledged and called upon) helps humanity move up the Attribute Ladder and live in closer alignment with God, as a reflection of God. To live more in alignment with our true nature, here and now, is the goal. The feelings of the internal desire to move back into alignment with God manifests in our lives as an internal tugging, or pulling, sensation in our hearts. These feelings can create a sense of longing and incompleteness, which are often mistaken for other things.

As long as you believe, and therefore operate from, a standpoint of separation, you will feel incomplete. When a shift in perspective causes a change in your perception, you will see that God is here, there, and everywhere. Then you will come to realize that you are complete and discover the whole you, just as you are.

Unlike the Lower Self, the Higher Self is aware of its sacred unity with God. The Higher Self knows that we have never been separate from God and that our perception of separation is only an illusion created by our minds.

How Does a Person Perceive and Connect with the Higher Self?

It would be fair to say that a part of our own journey through our various life experiences is to become aware of, perceive, connect with, and ultimately be in union with the Higher Self. For most people, the Higher Self remains in the background—not separate, but just observing what's going on. The Higher Self is quiet and still. It waits patiently for us to acknowledge its presence. When we consciously experience victories over the Lower Self, as well as when we learn to quiet our minds, the Higher Self moves forward out of the background and begins to come into our awareness.

Through the practice of quieting the conscious mind through meditation, pointing your intention toward developing greater awareness of God, and by living mindfully (thinking, feeling, and acting) consistently with the Higher Attributes, the Higher Self within you will move into the forefront of your mind.

To help clarify this point and demonstrate what this awareness may feel like, I'll share an excerpt taken from personal notes that I wrote after my first conscious experience of the Higher Self.

> *Last night during meditation, I became aware of a second thought, another thought not prompted by my own conscious thought. I can best describe it as when I am thinking, the thoughts originate in the middle to front part of my head. This new awareness of thought, however, was in the background, deeper within and towards the back of my head. It did not appear to be promoted by my mind. The thoughts (or awareness) of the presence were clear, but quiet. If I tried to consciously think about it, my own thoughts covered up the other. The thoughts that came deeper from within, toward the back of my head, by contrast seemed very serene and calm, like I had never experienced. It was as if this presence was observing me, watching and waiting in the background.*

Until we are ready to hear truth speaking its gentle whispers into our calm minds, the Higher Self, our divine watcher, observes and waits patiently—and non-judgmentally—as we journey into the illusions of the separate ego. The pathway to connectedness is a crooked and narrow path that we must make straight. We make the path straight and receive an increase in divine light, or spiritual nourishment, whenever we are victorious in a battle we face to raise our consciousness.

Our leader, the Higher Self, as a divine reflection of God, will lead us to experience the Higher Attributes in our day-to-day lives, as well as leading us towards recognition of the Kingdom of God. For, as Master Jesus said over and over, *"The kingdom of God is at hand."*

Attributes of the Higher Self, working through us, allow us to move forward in awareness and understanding of our oneness with God. The influence and perspective of the Higher Self allow us to *move away* from the "I, me, and mine" of life and *move toward* a larger, more expansive perspective of our daily interactions and relationships—one involving all of our thoughts, words, and actions.

Your understanding of how you can benefit from the influence and perspective of the Higher Self in your day-to-day life will be greatly enhanced when we discuss the Higher Attributes. For now, let us just stay with the idea that it is the guidance of the Higher Self that allows us to bring the attributes of our true, spiritual nature into our everyday experiences, helping us blend our humanity and spirituality into one experience.

Learning to Quiet the Mind

It is difficult, if not impossible, to perceive connection to the Higher Self with racing mental dialogue running non-stop. Stillness of mind is that which opens the gateway to the Higher Self.

Stillness of the mind begins with silence. We live in a loud, busy world, therefore, it is valuable for us to set aside time for internal and external silence during our day. The sun rises in the morning to bring in a new day in silence. The sun sets at the end of the day in silence. Is there any silence as you begin or end your day?

It is my observation that many people, from the time they wake up in the morning to the time they lay their heads down at night, experience a constant stream of noise. Some of this noise is external, but much is internal. Internal noise comes from mental chatter. It would appear that a large percentage of our population is uncomfortable being in silence, even for a short period of time. Or perhaps they've not yet recognized the value of *quieting the mind.*

If you feel this way, let me assure you that I'm not suggesting here that you must live like a monk in total silence. Certainly, there would be nothing wrong with that, if it were your path. However, I am merely suggesting that you consciously insert *some* silent time into your day. In Eckhart Tolle's book *The Power of Now* (New World Library, 1999), he states, *"Paying attention to the outer silence, creates inner silence, the mind becomes still."* I concur. At least initially, external silence will aid you in creating internal silence.

When you first begin to apply some silent time into your day purposefully, you may find that your mind doesn't know what to do or how to react. To compensate for this, your mind may race from topic to topic in order to fill the void of the internal silence. It may jump to things you need to do, or things you forgot to do, or to events that are coming up tomorrow or next week. In short, in the face of silence, the ego will kick and scream like a little child not getting its way.

Do not get frustrated. When you experience your mind drifting or racing, just bring it back to the present moment. Stay with the practice of slowing down the racing mind. Be fully conscious and aware in the present moment of the stillness. As you do this more often, you'll begin to notice that the racing, random thoughts of the mind slow down.

> *Whenever the mind wanders, restless and diffuse in its search for satisfaction without, lead it within; train it to rest in me* [God]. *Abiding joy comes to those who still the mind.* (The Bhagavad Gita 6:26–27)

In the Bible, we're shown Master Jesus regularly departing from his disciples to be alone to commune with God. What do you think he was doing in this time alone? I will submit that he was meditating. He was abiding in the stillness of his oneness with God. He constantly held himself in conscious connection with God. Notice how in certain passages he talks about God as though God was personally present. That's because God was, just as he is personally present with each and every one of us!

There *is* a place of stillness on the other side of the racing mind. It may take retraining of your mind for it to accept that it's okay for you just to *be* in the present moment. Once the mind understands and accepts this fact, you will find peace come to you in the space of no-mind, the absence of mental chatter.

The calm mind helps us not to *react* to circumstances or events in our lives, and it enables us to "pause" between the *stimulus* of events and our *response* to such events. It has been said that it does not matter *what* happens to us, but *how* we respond to what happens to us that matters most. This is true. Calming the mind makes us less reactive and more thoughtful in our choices.

As you practice and gain proficiency in calming your mind, you'll notice an increased amount of peace and calmness in your life. These will allow you to act and respond to life and life's experiences in a way that is more in alignment with the Higher Self.

We all lead busy lives. I know you may be wondering, *When on Earth will I be able to find time to quiet my mind?* I understand. Carving out silent time to still the mind won't happen automatically because you read this. However, this *is* achievable. You must make it happen. For some people, the best time for silence is in the morning; for others, it is the evening. Whenever it is for you, I assure you that after a short period of practice, you *will* notice a difference in your life! The difference that you notice will flow out of the ripples of peace and calmness in your mind, and also your heart, to touch every aspect of your physical, mental, emotional, and spiritual life.

Quieting the racing mind is one of the most important things you can do to begin to allow space for the Higher Self to guide you each step of the way towards victory over the Lower Self and claiming your divine inheritance.

CHAPTER 6
The Love-based Thought System

"Love is the beauty of the soul."
—Saint Augustine

Our habitual thoughts—whether we are conscious of them or not—occupy one of two thought systems: the love-based thought system or the fear-based thought system. In this chapter, we will look at the anatomy of the love-based thought system.

In all likelihood you have seen what happens when a pebble is dropped into a pool of water. The pebble enters the water and causes ripples to emanate in concentric circles around it. Let us call the pebble the "cause." Let us call the ripples the "effect." The ripples (the effect) move outward from their source (the cause) in both degree and relationship to the force of the pebble hitting the water.

Continuing with this analogy, let us say that the pebble is love. When love is brought out from within, and depending upon its degree, love will produce ripples in our energy field and manifest in our lives in a corresponding magnitude. It appears to be a rare occurrence that a person connects the ripples back to their original cause.

Everything vibrates according to its nature. Like all things, love has its own unique vibration.

Living in the Present Moment

Within the love-based thought system, the first ripple emanating outward from the love pebble into our lives is focusing or living in the *present moment*. Remember, at any given moment, there is only the present. For however long or briefly, I'm sure that at some point you've experienced the state of being entirely in the *present moment*. Have you ever been so into, so aware of, so engrossed in what was going on that you felt blissful and peaceful? During that experience, you completely lost track of time. Being in the present moment describes a state of *being*, not a method of thinking or acting.

One of the most effective ways of learning to just be in the *present moment* is the practice of meditation. By the way, I'm not suggesting that you can *only* experience the present moment while meditating, just that the art and practice of meditation allows us to become aware of our own thoughts and, more importantly, to slow down and still the racing mind. The racing mind will always try to take us down a path of recalling the past or projecting into the future. The greater degree with which we *observe* our own thoughts, the less likely it is that we'll become hostage to the reactive bombardment of the racing mind.

The present moment is all that we have. Everything takes place in the present—and this is where the Kingdom of God is. This is where the omnipresence of God can be realized: right here and right now.

Acceptance

The next ripple expanding outward in the love-based thought system is the ripple of *acceptance*. You may be thinking, *Acceptance of what or of whom?* The answer is acceptance of what *is*: acceptance of other people, and acceptance of events and situations. We can be observers of other people and situations. Period. We don't have to filter every situation through our own mental maps and then cast judgments upon it. By becoming conscious observers, we can train ourselves to stop one step short of judgment.

Please do not confuse acceptance with agreement. You can observe a situation or a person's behavior simply as what is. Observing without passing judgment does not by default mean that you agree with the situation, event, or behavior. But the constant judging of others, and the corresponding need to try to change them, creates much internal strife and disharmony in your life.

Acceptance of what is, as an *observer*, will become easier as your awareness and consciousness expands. As your state and level of awareness expands, you'll begin to see a much larger picture of life. You can begin to see that all things happen for their own reasons. You can begin to have the awareness that everything is perfect just the way it is. It does not mean that this represents ultimate perfection; but that, for this moment, things are the way they are—and moving toward perfection.

Acceptance takes on the form of surrendering to what is. Surrendering takes strength and courage. Acceptance (at least initially) takes your conscious attention; it is by no means passive. You can surrender to, and accept what is and still take action in any given situation. But the action you take is not a judgment. The action has to do with your own choices, not with judging others or portraying negative emotions toward them.

Acceptance, and surrendering to what is means we acknowledge the fact that we see things only from our own limited perspective. We acknowledge the fact that we don't know the journey of another person's soul, nor do we know the path, the successes, the errors, or the karmic interrelationship dance between other souls, therefore, how could we ever judge them?

Acceptance flows out of, and takes on, both the position of surrendering and acknowledging that God's perspective of this life's dance is far more complete than our own perspective.

Abundance

The next ripple flowing out of the love-based thought system is the ripple of *abundance*. The greatest abundance that we could ever ask for in our earthly lives is an abundance of peace, an abundance of realization of our oneness with the presence of God. This abundance is a deep, all-encompassing feeling of peaceful joy that permeates our being when we live in awareness of oneness with God.

Abundance of peace can be realized when we live within the love-based thought system, living in the present moment and embracing everything with acceptance. Conflict, turmoil, suffering, and negative vibrations (all types of energy created in error), become extinguished by the light of the higher vibrations of love and the corresponding ripples that flow out of love.

Abundance embraces the thoughts and feelings (and beliefs) that there is enough of something to go around. An abundance mindset will assist you in manifesting all that you need in your life.

> *Or who is the man among you, who when his son asks him for bread, will hand him a stone? Or if he should ask him for fish, will he hand him a snake? If therefore you who err, know how to give good gifts to your sons, how much more will your Father in Heaven give good things to those who ask him?* (Matthew 7:9–11)

The abundance I am speaking of goes far beyond the basic needs in life of food, air, water, shelter, and clothing. The law of thought and manifestation can apply to abundance in friendships, kindness, courage, strength, love, and financial means.

Being the polar opposite of the habitual thought process of lack and limitation, the ripples of an abundant mindset (which I define as a group of beliefs) creates their own vibrations surrounding and emanating outward from an individual. Abundance thought vibrations open us up and inform God's infinite universe of possibilities that we're preparing ourselves to receive.

As God's children, equipped with a growing realization of who we really are, we can embrace this conscious way of being as we proceed through the battles of the Divine Child, and ultimately emerge victorious over the Lower Self, on our path to the Kingdom of God.

Certainly there are many more ripples that flow outward from love than the few highlighted above. As we move into discussing the Higher Attributes in more detail later on, you'll see that we could say that *all* of the Higher Attributes flow originally out of love.

> *Teacher, which is the greatest commandment in the Law? Jesus said to him, Love the Lord your God with all your heart and with all your soul and with all your might and with all of your mind. This is the greatest and first commandment. And the second is like to it, Love your neighbor as yourself.* (Matthew 22:36–39)

PART THREE

Obstacles on the Path to Victory

"Each of us is something of a schizophrenic personality, tragically divided against ourselves."

—Martin Luther King, Jr.

CHAPTER 7

The Lower Self

"Experience: that most brutal of teachers.
But you learn, my God do you learn."
—C.S. Lewis

I n John 8:32, it is written, *"You will know the truth, and that very truth will make you free."* The part of this statement that is not talked about very often is that although the truth *will* set you free, in the process you can become very uncomfortable. Most people prefer to operate their lives within a *comfort zone*, rather than to become temporarily uncomfortable, even when the reward after the period of discomfort is great. Learning about truths of the Lower Self has the potential to cause some form of discomfort, while at the same time it can set you free.

The path of the battles of Divine Child is a life transforming path. To experience transformation involves change, among other things. Change can be very exciting, but it can also cause discomfort. For now, I encourage you just to observe any discomfort you experience, but don't react to it. If you feel discomfort, you may ask yourself these questions:

- Where does this discomfort come from?
- Who is the one causing this discomfort to surface?

Two Selves occupy all people. These two Selves have specific, yet very different characteristics. We will identify, define, and explore these characteristics in some depth now. It is important to have a working understanding of the aspects of the two Selves as we move forward.

The two Selves are the separate ego (the Lower Self) and the indivisible Atman (the Higher Self).

> *When One rises above I and me and mine, The Atman is revealed as one's real Self.* (Katha Upanishad 2.3:13)

Who and What Is the Lower Self?

The Lower Self, or the ego self, is the separate identity that identifies itself with words such as "I," "me," and "mine," and as an individual body and mind of a person. The Lower Self identifies itself with the physical body and that individual personality that inhabits the body, and is not aware of sacred unity or its true nature.

The ego self is the impermanent illusion through which most people operate and govern their lives. The ego self believes and has fully identified itself as an individual being separate from God. The belief in separation originates from the perspective that "I am right here, living, breathing, thinking, and acting in the world, whereas God is someplace else, far above and far away." The ego self says, "Hey, I sense this world around me through my eyes, ears, nose, taste, and touch as a separate being." Because the ego self fully identifies itself with the body it experiences and perceives itself as having a separate existence from God.

Functioning within many people, the Lower Self has forgotten, thus is unaware of, its oneness with God as it is manifested through the Divine Child. Because the ego self has forgotten its true nature, it therefore creates a separate identity of its own.

The ego self, of its own accord, does not automatically seek to know or remember the experience of sacred unity. This is largely because moving toward God is outside of the boundaries of that which the five senses report back to the ego self as *reality*. Essentially, the creation of the illusion of an existence apart from God is, in large part, a result of what the five senses report back to us and which we thus can interpret as finite reality.

Here is an analogy for the ego self. Imagine being the ego self, the one in charge of running your thoughts and feelings, your reactions to life experience, and you know that your days are numbered. That is, you have a finite existence. Your existence is based on the perceptions of an illusion of what is real. Now imagine that the ego self knows a secret (and it is not telling you what it is). The secret is that the ego's finite existence, its life expectancy, if you will, is even shorter when you become at-one with the Higher Self. In this case, the Higher Self, representing our true nature and rooted in the eternal, will rule, giving the ego self a back seat. To the ego this is the same as dying! It fears at-onement.

So you could say this is a survival game for the ego: a battle between the ego and the spirit. I am sure your ego self will be very upset with me for telling you what's really going on. In this battle, the ego self has a few powerful key weapons in its arsenal to support its lifespan and survival. We'll explore these key weapons in just a moment.

For now, my friend, trust me when I say that the Lower Self won't give up, nor give in easily as you move forward allowing the Higher Self to enter the forefront of your life. This inner work can, at times, be some of the hardest work you will face. It is during these difficult times that the Lower Self can feel or appear to be the enemy. But rest assured, the Lower Self is playing a role in leading you to have the experiences your soul desires. It is in this light that I hope and pray this information can assist you on your journey through the Seven Victories of the Divine Child.

How Does the Lower Self Function?

You may ask, "If the Lower Self represents less desirable aspects of me, then why did God create or allow the Lower Self to exist?" This is a great question. First, understand that God did not create the aspects of the Lower Self, human beings have. However, there are actually benefits that the Lower Self provides.

The Lower Self provides us with the opportunity to experience that which we are not. It is through experiencing what we are not that we can *fully experience* and, in turn, *know* what and who we really are.

You see, it's one thing for our soul to *know* what and who we are not; it's an entirely different thing to *experience* what and who we are not. One possible comparison of this point—*of knowing vs. experiencing*—would be similar to reading about something in a book on, for example, rock climbing. We could read all about rock climbing and talk to others who have rock climbed, to the point that we may feel we know all about rock climbing. But the real experience of actually rock climbing for the first time would be very different than just reading about it. Experiencing something is far more valuable than just knowing about it conceptually.

The Lower Self provides us with a relative experience, in a dualistic world, so that we may know—through the experience of them—our real, Higher-self aspects of God. You see, if all we ever knew were the divine aspects of God, we couldn't recognize them because we wouldn't know anything else. We can only recognize pure light and pure love by having experiences that are the opposite of these Higher Attributes.

All our Lower Attributes arise from the illusion of our separation from God, and consequently, from the forgetfulness of our true nature. *This illusion is only a perception.* Our perceptions, at any moment, are a result of our current beliefs. The illusion of our separation from God begins to dissolve in *the very moment* that a person chooses to change his or her perceptions of his or her relationship with God.

We live in the illusion of separation when we completely identify ourselves with our physical body and our five senses. When the mind is trapped within the perceived confines of the physical body, our five senses provide us with stimulus and feedback, but only from the limited world that our eyes can see, our ears can hear, our hands can touch, and so on. We conclude that this experience is *mine*, and therefore, the presence of God must be somewhere else.

Based on observation, I suggest that a majority of people operate their lives from the illusionary state of being separate from God. This goes far beyond simply *believing in God*. One can strongly believe in God and still live in the illusion of being separate from God. In reality, the walls of separation do not exist. They only exist because we've put them there, or because we allow others to erect the walls for us. The walls of separation—being only an illusion—begin to crumble the moment we choose to see that God is right here right now.

When we choose to see God as a part of us, inside and outside (meaning, when we choose to see God as all that there is), we come to the place where we consciously realize that it's impossible to live outside of, or separated from God. Simply put, nothing can exist outside of all that there is.

For many people, the process of dissolving the illusion of separation occurs over a period of time. We set the dissolving process in motion when *a conscious will to change* the way we view God is present. When we change our perception of God from one of God sitting in some far off place called "heaven," into a perception of God being right here right now, woven into the very fabric of life and consciousness itself, the illusion of separation begins to vanish.

We can move forward into the perspective that we live, move, and experience our being inside of God and God inside of us. In essence, we are rewriting our conscious and subconscious minds, allowing new truths to replace old assumptions, those things which in the past we had accepted as true.

Do not imitate the way of this world, but be transformed by the renewing of your minds. (Romans 12:2)

What Is the Purpose of the Lower Self?

The Lower Self plays a role—for a time—in assisting us with the life experiences we need (or you could say the experiences we've chosen!) for ourselves in order to remember and personally experience the Higher Attributes, ways of being and qualities within us that are clearer reflections of our true, spiritual nature.

The separate identity of the ego occupies the mind with thoughts of the past—hurts and pains—and provides a steady stream of hypothetical thoughts of the future. The ego finds it difficult to spend any more than a fraction of its effort in the present moment.

As a result of its past/future orientation, the Lower Self can breed fear. Arising out of fear, come the Lower Attributes of a sense of separation, guilt, anger, hatred, judgment, selfishness, resentment, and other harmful, disharmonious thoughts and feelings. These Lower Attributes can (and do) manifest in three forms: thoughts, words, and actions.

As previously stated, none of this suggests that the Lower Self, the ego, is inherently bad. The ego, our individual identification of who we *think* we are as separate beings, serves a purpose in helping our soul experience the duality of material life and in accomplishing a majority of our chosen life lessons. The objective, however, is to transform the Lower Self with the Higher Self. *The two must become as one.* The goal is to begin to function and live our lives from merging the ego with the Higher Self while still on Earth in the physical body.

When the attributes of the Lower Self have been transmuted or changed into love and other, corresponding Higher Attributes, the "savior," the Higher Self, will reign in our hearts and in our minds.

There is no value is cursing the Lower Self and its manifestations; instead, we must acknowledge life's experiences for what they are: opportunities to experientially know the Higher Attributes. The notion of this will come to life more as you read through the chapters on the battles and victories of the Divine Child in Part Five.

As noted earlier, the ego has a few key weapons in its arsenal that support its lifespan and survival. Its main weapons are fear and guilt, both of which can (and do) cause havoc in people's lives. Not to mention, both fear and guilt are totally made up and exist only in our minds. At the core, fear and guilt, and the manifestations that consequently flow from them, are choices—albeit choices that are usually made unconsciously. Just as fear and guilt are choices, so is self-mastery a choice. We can work from the perspective of self-mastery and consciously make different choices.

Fear and guilt have no lives of their own, aside from the energy that we ourselves give to them in our own thoughts.

CHAPTER 8
The Ego's Weapon of Fear

"If a man harbors any sort of fear, it percolates through all thinking, damages his personality and makes him a landlord to a ghost."
—Lloyd Douglas

R*ANDOM* H*OUSE* U*NABRIDGED* D*ICTIONARY* defines fear as "a distressing emotion aroused by impending danger, evil, pain, etc., whether the threat is real or imagined."

Fear (which is an acronym for False Experiences Appearing Real) causes emotions and behaviors that are rarely traced back to their true source. Fear causes people to curse the past by replaying it over and over in their minds. Fear also causes people to dread the future by rehearsing made-up scenarios in their minds. Most of these made-up scenarios, if not all of them, have less than pleasant outcomes, of which 99 percent will never come to pass. However, all the while people worry, the ego is behind the scenes running the show.

I am sure that you've experienced fear of something about the future that never came to pass. Time, energy, and emotions were wasted as you focused on an illusion, were they not?

You may find it challenging to relate issues in your day-to-day life to the word "fear." If you find my use of the word "fear" is a stumbling block here, substitute words for fear that have less intensity. Close relatives are the words "worry" and "anxiety."

A vast majority of the fears, worries, and anxieties people feel and experience day to day can be grouped under the heading "fear of the unknown." Fear, worry, and anxiety are future-based "what ifs" projecting out into some unknown time. Most everything in our material life that extends beyond the present moment is unknown. This is part of what makes life so exciting!

We possess an interesting sorting mechanism in our thought processes that determines what we choose to focus our energies on. We do not fear everything in the future, even though most everything is unknown. We sort and choose particular parts of our unknown future to be concerned about. For example, as I am sitting at my desk writing these sentences, I have no concerns or fears in this moment. As my children are playing in the next room, I have no fears for them in this moment. But if I allow myself to project myself into the future, I could find something that is clearly unknown to me to be concerned about in this moment.

Not many people want to say this, but here it is: What I am really saying when I fear something in my unknown future is that my trust is low. My trust in God's divine plan, my trust in God's presence guiding me, leading me, is low. The fact is, if at any moment I trusted my Divine Parents and their guidance and support through my life enough, how could I fear anything … including death? What would there be to fear?

So in those times when I catch myself being too anxious, too concerned, or even fearful about something in the unknown future, I realize in that moment that I must pause and reassess my level of trust. My fears are made up and God is real! I can acknowledge that my trust in God is greater than my made-up fear. In reality, I have nothing to fear.

When I pause and remind myself of this, in that moment, I can feel my anxiety, tension, and uneasiness simply melting away.

Consider this, have you ever felt or heard others say something that sounded like, "My mind won't stop racing" or "I can't quiet my mind, it just keeps going"? If people cannot quiet their own minds, who is running the show? The ego.

At the most conscious level, we have the ability to control and direct our own thoughts. The ego causes the mind to race and ramble endlessly. It does this just to stay in control, because it knows that there is truth in the phrase "Be still and know that I am God." The stillness this phrase is referring to is the stillness of the mind, or more accurately the stillness of the racing, anxious, and reactive thoughts of the restless mind. The ego knows that when the mind slows down, and becomes quiet, the still small voice of the Higher Self within can be detected.

For this reason, the ego doesn't want you to stop or pause to think objectively about your own thoughts. It would prefer that you continue just to *react* unconsciously to whatever stimulation it feeds your racing mind.

It is a known fact that you can change your physiology, simply by changing your thoughts. However, to accomplish this, you must first become self-aware, or conscious of your thoughts, and separate the thoughts themselves from the *thinker* of the thoughts. Then you'll be able to observe your thoughts objectively and be able to "push the pause button" in order to allow yourself the space and freedom to choose different thoughts. This is a critical skill that may need to be developed, much like developing a muscle.

In a moment, we will move forward in our discussion on changing polarity between the Lower Attributes and the Higher Attributes; for now, take note that this skill of being able to "push the pause button" on your thoughts, in order to choose different thoughts, will serve you quite well.

You may find it helpful to think about fear from the standpoint that it exists as a tool to provide you with the opportunity to choose to move towards its opposite, which, of course, is love. I realize that this may be easier said than done in practice. To help you, we will be going into more depth on moving from fear to love in subsequent chapters.

Because fear is imagined and has no roots in the reality of who you are, you may dissolve any fears in your life once you fully realize that you're no longer in need of the experiences that fear provides.

Fear can only spring to life when we are replaying the past and projecting made-up scenarios or outcomes into the future. Fear does not exist in the *present moment*. Fear has no home in the heart and mind of God's Divine Child. This means you!

CHAPTER 9
The Ego's Weapon of Guilt

"Change your thoughts and you change your world."
—Norman Vincent Peale

RANDOM HOUSE UNABRIDGED DICTIONARY defines guilt as "a feeling of responsibility or remorse for some offense, crime, wrong, etc., whether real or imagined." Notice how it reads: *"Real or imagined."*

Let us first recognize that *guilt* is an effect of some other cause. Guilt does not show up of its own accord. Guilt shows up as a result of something else that's real or imagined. It is very difficult to overcome, eliminate, or release guilt by attacking the guilty feeling itself. This would be equivalent to trying to cut down a tree by pulling off its leaves. Instead, we must first go to the root cause of the guilt, and then we can see guilt for what it is: an illusion.

Guilt comes from the ego into our minds; it does not come from God. Occupying the mind with guilt, and all the thoughts and emotions that flow out of guilt, is yet another distraction the ego uses to stay in control of the mind to ensure its survival.

Guilt is an ego-imposed state of mind. When we cut through the smoke and mirrors of guilt, we can see that the thoughts and emotions that appeared to ignite guilt were all made up. When our self-awareness "muscles" strengthen, we find that we're less apt to fall into the default pattern of simply *reacting* to the unconscious flow of our thoughts and emotions. Being aware of our thoughts and emotions empowers us to be able to "push the pause button" on the racing mind. It is within the space of the calm mind that we have the freedom to question the mind and potentially choose a different perspective. At any moment, we have the freedom to choose a different way of viewing any situation.

When we ask, "Who is making me feel this guilt?" we begin a process of unraveling the illusion of our guilt. If our initial answer to this question is, "Someone else" (that is, "So-and-so is making me feel guilty"), we need to put on the brakes and stop our thought process right then and there. No one else can *make us* feel guilty, until and unless *we allow* his or her potential efforts to succeed.

You may say, "Well I don't allow So-and-so to make me feel guilty, he/she just does!" Not so. While it may be the case that So-and-so is *trying* to make you feel guilty (consciously or unconsciously), his/her efforts at *trying* to make you feel guilty are totally different than you allowing his/her efforts to have an effect on you. In other words, you have a choice! It is as simple as that (but perhaps not easy). You have a choice!

No longer do we just have to *react* to past patterns of what the ego feeds into our minds. When we slow down the racing, anxious, and reactive mind, we gain a sense of freedom and peace that comes into our awareness through knowing that we can choose what and how we think and feel.

Turning our attention back to the self-imposed question asked earlier, "Who is making me feel this guilt?" Let us say, in a new example, that your answer to the question is, "I am making myself feel guilty." Who is the "I" in the answer? Is it the "I" of the individual ego (the Lower Self), or the "I" of the Higher Self?

It may be helpful to think about it this way. We can determine the type of tree by the nature of its fruit. If we see apples on a tree, then we know the tree has to be an apple tree. If the fruit is a Lower

Attribute (in this case, guilt), then the tree from which it hangs is the tree of the Lower Self. If the fruit is a Higher Attribute, such as forgiveness, then the tree on which the fruit of forgiveness hangs is the tree of the Higher Self. Once again, we can determine the type of tree by the nature of its fruit. In our life's experiences, we're in a seemingly constant process (or battle) of moving from Lower Attributes to Higher Attributes.

If and when guilt is experienced, if it's not transmuted from its Lower Attribute state into a Higher Attribute state, the guilt can take on a life of its own: A person could hang on to guilt for weeks, months, and even, in some cases, years. The guilt that a person has kept alive for months or years can become so attached to the person that he or she identifies and perhaps even defines who he/she thinks he/she is around the guilt. By this time, it is likely that the initial feeling of guilt evolved into other thought and feeling forms, such as unhappiness, blame, resentment, and anger.

Guilt stays alive only by us living in the past. Guilt has no life of its own when we live in the present moment. The good news is, remembering that the guilt originally started as a made-up illusion, it's never too late to make the choice of cutting down the guilt tree. We can cut down the guilt tree, essentially dissolving guilt into its opposite by applying the Principle of Polarity. (We will be discussing how to apply the Principle of Polarity in Part Five).

Please remember, all the while you are going through the dramas of life that you create, your true nature (the Atman, the Christ, the Higher Self within) remains untouched by the unfolding of life's play and the vast illusions of fear and guilt.

CHAPTER 10

The Fear-based Thought System

"Man stands in his own shadow and wonders why it's dark."
—Zen Proverb

A FEAR-BASED THOUGHT SYSTEM is largely an unconscious method or process of thinking. Seldom do we question our own thoughts, and therefore they flow out of past patterns of thinking, or prior mental mapping.

Neuroscience suggests that our patterns of thinking are developed when the same sequence of neurons is fired in the brain over and over, producing specific thoughts and emotions. The patterns or sequences in which neurons are fired the most often over time can begin to fire automatically with little initial stimulus. For example, if a person has formed a habitual pattern of judging others, the pathway of all the neurons that connect to form the judgmental thoughts become well worn compared to the pathways, let's say, of acceptance, which could, but may not be used as often. The neural pathways that produce thoughts of acceptance are in fact less worn if they are less traveled.

It may be helpful to liken the neural pathways we create to creating a path through the woods. When the same place is traveled over and over, it becomes a well-worn path, easier to travel. There are few or no obstructions, so the way is clear. Compare this to walking through the woods, through grass or brush, a different way each time: In this case, no clear path of travel is worn into the terrain.

The more worn neural pathways are—as they are with our habitual patterns of thinking—the more likely we will follow that same way of thinking unconsciously. Our habitual patterns of thinking happen so quickly that we no longer notice or question them.

Thought patterns that have been habitually formed can be triggered instantly, and unconsciously, so we no longer even realize we're thinking in a certain way. To change patterns of thinking from being judgmental, for example, to thoughts of acceptance, we have to consciously choose the new way of thinking in order to *form new pathways*, and do so repeatedly until they, too, become well worn. If we don't choose a different way of thinking consciously, it is natural to fall back into our well-worn patterns, which if they are run by the ego are typically based on fear. Our current, well-worn patterns of thinking may or may not be serving our highest and best good at the present moment.

We must become self-aware and conscious of our thoughts and feelings in order to realize their current existence. Using the example given above, if through becoming more self-aware a person realized that he or she judged events and other people, he or she could catch him or herself in the middle of the process of judging. The individual could simply "push the pause button" on his or her thoughts right then and there, and in the quietness of the pause, have the complete freedom to choose a different way of thinking. The individual then may choose to change his or her thinking from judging to acceptance.

We accomplish transformation in thought, at least initially, by asking ourselves a question in the space created by the pause in our thinking. We ask, "How can I view or change my perception of this event or of this person?" It is through the act of pausing and asking ourselves whether or not our current way of viewing a situation serves our highest and best good that we allow space for the Divine within to guide our daily human experiences.

At the risk of getting ahead of myself, let me reiterate that *asking ourselves questions* opens up the doorway to allow the Higher Self to guide us in finding the answers we need for our self-imposed questions. This is both a secret revealed and a pathway to peace.

Earlier, when discussing the love-based thought system, we used the analogy of dropping a pebble into a pool of water. The ripples produced by the pebble (the cause) hitting the water (the effect) extend out from their source in the same degree as the force of the pebble hitting the water. The effect is related to the cause.

Continuing with this analogy, let us say that the pebble we drop in the water of our consciousness is not a pebble of love, but a pebble of fear and guilt. As fear and guilt enter our awareness, depending on their magnitude they will produce ripples of different degrees in our lives. It appears to be a rare occurrence that a person connects the effects of negativity, pain, and suffering, back to the cause of fear and guilt.

Living in the Past or in the Future

The first ripples that are an effect of the fear/guilt pebble are the tendency to focus our thoughts and therefore our energy on *living in the past* (guilt-driven thoughts) or on *living in the future* (fear-driven thoughts). Both of these focuses are distractions produced by the ego that cause a person not to live in the present, which is always free of fear and guilt.

Remember, the ego's mission is to stay in control of the mind. It accomplishes this by having us *constantly* living where we are not: in the past or in the future. Only in our memory and imagination can we live in the past or in the future. At any given moment, however, there really is *only the present*. The present is what is.

Living in the past is different than *learning from the past*. We can learn from our past without allowing our thoughts to create guilty feelings in us, and without dwelling there. In the past, we may have exhibited thoughts, words, or actions that flowed out of the attributes of the Lower Self, but what value is there in constantly replaying or beating ourselves up over these past errors? We can learn from the past by adjusting our thoughts, words, and actions toward exhibition of Higher Attributes.

If we repeat the same errors over and over, this means we simply haven't yet learned what we need to learn from our experiences. Learning is about adjusting and changing. What is past is past. Now you can change the pebbles that create your future.

Think about it this way: God and everything in your life are here right now. When you change the *quality and nature* of your pebble—away from fear and guilt—you immediately change the *quality and nature* of the ripples in your life.

We Give Everything Meaning

The next ripple caused by the fear/guilt pebble is *judgment*. What is it to be judgmental? Being judgmental is the act of comparing something or someone to a standard or basis that we have accepted, or *perceived*, as right or true. Judgment flows out of our limited, finite perspective of an individual soul's journey.

Many people are in a constant state of judging events and people. At the same time, many people are their own worst critics: judging themselves too harshly. What drives these behaviors? Who is doing the judging? Once again, we find the Lower Self, the ego self at work trying to help us make sense of the world. When the ego prompts us to focus our attention on judging others, it once again stays in control.

In Part Four, we'll review tools and applications for reducing and ultimately eliminating judgment. However, for the time being, try this. Go one full day without judgment or being judgmental of another.

If you catch yourself judging, stop and become aware of what's happening. You may find it helpful to just pause and ask, "What value or purpose does this judgment serve?" In all likelihood, you'll find that the answer to your own question will be, "None." The judgment serves no value.

It is important to see the difference between observation and judgment. You can observe what *is*, and use it to make discernments, without turning your pure observation into a judgment. Don't rationalize. Be true to yourself. Everything in life just is. We give everything meaning. Our perception of the *meaning* we assign is just that: our perception. Our perceptions will be different if we are coming from a Lower Attribute perspective versus a Higher Attribute perspective. The event itself does not change, only how we perceive it changes.

Catching ourselves judging is the first step in curing ourselves of this tendency. You will find as your self-awareness increases (and it won't take long) that you'll become very sensitive, perhaps even a bit uneasy, when you're in the presence of someone being judgmental of another. The energy created by judgment will feel disharmonious because it carries its own distinct vibration.

> *Judge not, that you may not be judged. For the same judgment that you judge, you will be judged.* (Matthew 7:1–2)

As it relates to judging, the fact of the matter is that until we have the knowledge and wisdom of God's divine plan for other people's lives we aren't in any position to judge them correctly. Life's tapestry is being woven perfectly by God to accomplish each soul's journey back to oneness with God. We do not know all of the details, so why judge?

Scarcity or a Feeling of Lack

After judgment, the next ripple caused by the fear/guilt pebble is *scarcity* or a *feeling of lack and limitation*. Scarcity is the feeling or perception that there isn't enough of something to go around. Our feelings or perceptions of lack may come in the form of a sense of lack of love, peace, security, happiness, money, time, and so forth.

When a person has a scarcity mentality then there is more of a perceived need to *get* what he or she feels is lacking rather than to *give*. If someone believes there's only so much to go around, that person would need to spend time and energy acquiring enough for his or herself, through selfish acts of taking care of *number one*, until a point in time when the person feels he or she has *enough* of something (which rarely ever happens). *Then* the person feels he or she will be in a position to give in order to help others. But this is *always* at a later date.

The truth of the matter is that the universe works on a formula that says, "We get by giving." So if there is something we want, we can obtain it by giving the same away, allowing the door to open for us to receive more.

If you want more friends, be a good friend. If you want more kindness in your life, be kind. If you want more love in your life, give away more love, and so on. Although this may be counter intuitive, this is how things work. God's laws often work in reverse of human logic. And yes, until you personally experience the power of giving in your life, it may be hard to believe in it. However, once you have experienced it, your faith will be transformed into pure knowing.

The things in life that most people would label as *problems* are, in fact, *opportunities* in disguise. These opportunities act as open doors, allowing us to reach inside to access the part of us that is higher than our ego and stands above our hurts and pains, so that we may pull aspects of the Divine into our human experience.

PART FOUR

Universal Wisdom Tools
of the Divine Child

*"Intuition is a spiritual faculty and does
not explain, but simply points the way."*

—Florence Scovel Shinn

CHAPTER 11

The Power of Thought and Creative Energy

"As a man thinketh in his heart, so is he."
—Proverbs 23:7

BEFORE WE PROCEED DIRECTLY into a discussion of the battles of the Divine Child, it is appropriate to spend time reviewing some concepts and tools that will assist you in being victorious. These include: thought and creative energy, prayer, meditation, and self-mastery. Practical application of these tools in everyday life fertilizes the soil on which victory takes place.

It is highly likely that at some point you've heard or read the phrase, "Thoughts are things." What, specifically, does this mean? To start, let's look to *The Book of Genesis,* which tells us that in this beginning there was nothing. Then, through the *thoughts* of the creative aspects of God, which are known in Hebrew as the Elohim (meaning the one and the many), all things were created. This process continues. Creation begins mentally, with thought, then thoughts manifest into physical form. This is the principle of *mentalism.*

Through the principle of mentalism, we act as co-creators with God. All of us have co-created many things in our lives that did not exist in the past. None of these things were created without it first beginning in the form of a thought.

Due to the apparent delay in time (as we know it) between our thoughts and the creation that comes into being from those thoughts, many of us don't see the connection between the thought and its creation. Thoughts are causes; the outcomes of thoughts are effects. As we saw when we looked at the love-based and fear-based thought systems, thoughts are our pebbles dropping into water, and their effects are the ripples emanating from the thoughts. The further in time the cause (thought) is separated from the effect (result of the thought), the less likely we are to perceive the connection between the two. When we don't make a connection, these two aspects of creation feel like entirely separate events in our life.

Energy follows thought. All states of mind produce outcomes in our external world that mirror our internal world. By not seeing the connection between a cause and its corresponding effect, a person often looks at outcomes in disbelief, or cries out, "How could this have happened to me?"

What we fill our subconscious mind with either suddenly or gradually begins to manifest on the unseen plane. As the direction to the subconscious mind continues and strengthens (backed by belief), the manifestation grows into its creative fulfillment in the material world. Therefore it's important for us to recognize that if we do not run our subconscious minds ourselves, and become the gatekeeper for what goes into it, someone else will run it for us.

If we desire to lead love-based lives, we must learn to consciously choose the direction that we want the energy of our conscious and subconscious minds to work toward. Here are four ways to do so.

- Think and speak of solutions, not problems
- Think and speak of health, not sickness

- Think and speak of opportunity and joyful acts, not loss and failure
- Think and speak of abundance, not lack

If you'd like a visional representation of the creative power of thought, picture the head of a person, as thoughts are occurring. Visualize the thoughts as waves of energy flowing out of the top of the head and being projected out into the space around the thinking person—and beyond. As thought vibrations project outward from us, they attract back into our lives experiences that are a reflection of those thoughts. This is known as the *law of attraction*.

Let's review an example from each of the thought systems we previously discussed (the fear-based thought system and the love-based thought system) in order to study how they relate to the power of thought and creative energy. Starting with the fear-based thought system, imagine that the dominant thoughts a person has are thoughts of fear, guilt, judgment, and lack. As these radiate or vibrate outward from the individual, through the law of attraction this individual either suddenly or gradually begins to find that events begin or continue *(if it has been going on for some time)* to occur in his or her life that correspond to, and are the *effect* of those very thoughts.

You see, the universe is perfect, balanced, and just. God is perfect and so the universe God created is perfect. There is no punishment. Flowing out of spiritual law, there are only natural consequences (pleasant or unpleasant) of our own thoughts, words, and actions. The universe gives us exactly what we ask for; only many times the asking is not performed at a conscious level. Nevertheless, because the universe seeks to maintain balance, events occur in our lives that are consistent with our dominant thoughts.

Have you ever known someone who always appears to have things that may be labeled as "unfortunate" happen to him or her? Now this could be a very nice person, but I would ask: What is the makeup of the thoughts that run through the individual's mind on a regular basis? What are we attracting into our lives when our thoughts occupy fear, guilt, judgment, or lack? The short answer is: more of the same.

Knowing the thoughts of another person is not for us to know; only God knows. This is why we are in no position to judge anyone. The question we need to ask of ourselves is: How are we using our God-given creative energy?

> *I am he who searches the minds and hearts; and I will give to everyone of you according to your works.* (Revelations 2:23)

Now let's turn our attention to studying the creations produced by an individual whose dominate thoughts occupy the love-based thought system. The vibrations of thoughts of love, kindness, selfless service, acceptance, and abundance project out into the universe around the person and return to the person in the form of events or circumstances that are consistent with those thoughts. Once again, in fulfillment of spiritual laws, thoughts return more of the same. This is the law of attraction and the law of cause and effect in action. We are in a constant state of attracting vibrations into our lives that are consistent with the pattern of our dominant thoughts.

You can see the importance of being aware of *what* and *how* we are thinking: Our thoughts *will* determine our reality. Because we understand spiritual law, we can purposefully make different choices in our lives that flow in harmony with our true spiritual nature—the Higher Self—and God's divine will for our lives, which is to remember our oneness with God.

Having come to recognize the fact that your dominant thoughts create your reality, you will see by extension, that how you habitually feel (your emotions), the words you speak, and the actions you take are the keys to creating ideal life circumstances and, in some cases, changing your life circumstances. If you are attracting circumstances into your life consistent with your predominant thoughts, it would stand to reason that if you want to improve your life you can begin by changing what you think about.

We come to understand the meaning behind Norman Vincent Peale's statement when he said, "Change your thoughts and you can change your life." The exciting point to grasp is that you have the power and control over your own thoughts, and, therefore, can change your own thoughts affecting your own reality. You are not a prisoner to your thoughts unless you allow them to run unchecked. Nor are the events or circumstances in your life a punishment from God. They are simply a fulfillment of the law of cause and effect.

There is power in choosing/creating your thoughts; and God has also given you the will power to think about, and be aware of your own thoughts, and shift their energy. If your thoughts don't serve you and your highest good—flowing from the Higher Self—then you have the opportunity and choice to change them.

As I live, says the Lord, as you have spoken in my presence, so I will do to you. (Numbers 14:28)

An analogy may help you become self-aware of how you think. Imagine that you have a "special pillow." Connected to this pillow is a cord attached to a printer. Each night when you lay your head down on your special pillow to go to sleep, you push a button. The printer begins to print out all the thoughts you had throughout the day. In the morning when you wake up, you have a printout of pages upon pages of thoughts you had the prior day. What would be the dominant theme of the thoughts as you read your printout? Would you be reading about thoughts that occupy the fear-based system? Or would you be reading about thoughts that occupy the love-based system?

Think about your thoughts today. Are your thoughts generally positive and supportive as if they come from the mind of the Higher Self? Or are your thoughts largely negative and self-defeating as if coming from the Lower Self? Either way, the wonderful thing to remember is that whether you like or dislike what you read on your "printout" tomorrow, you have both the ability and the choice to keep your thoughts the same or to change them. You, indeed, have free will. It's up to you to choose how you think.

What we're talking about here is self-awareness. Being self-aware and adjusting our thoughts, words, and actions to bring them into better alignment with the Higher Self (the Divine within us) is a component of self-mastery: Mastery over our own thoughts and, therefore, mastery over our own emotions, ultimately gives us mastery of our own lives. Self-mastery is about taking personal responsibility for our lives.

Each of us is starting from exactly where we are right now. So whether self-mastery of your thoughts, which will lead you to greater control of your emotions, is easy or difficult for you depends entirely on your current level of self-awareness. Either way, easy or difficult, you can do it!

Remember, energy follows thought. You can be resurrected—made anew—by raising your thoughts, words, and actions to the level of the Higher Attributes.

CHAPTER 12

The Power of Prayer

"Good morning God, Thy will be done,
Today is a day of completion,
Miracle will follow miracle,
And wonders will never cease."
—Florence Scovel Shinn

WHAT IS PRAYER? *The Aquarian Gospel of Jesus the Christ* (94:2) gives us the following definition.

Prayer is the deep communion of the soul with God.

How many people have been taught how to pray, the value of prayer, or the power of prayer? Were you? And I am not talking about reciting prayers by rote that you were taught as a child. Reciting prayers from memory with little to no thought, feeling, and energy behind the prayer may not yield the desired communion with God.

So what is an effective way to pray? First, prayer requires having faith. It is fair to say that our level of faith in prayer has much to do with our individual experiences and our belief that our prayers are being heard, as in how we define the fulfillment of prayers. It is likely that most of us have experiences of prayers being answered, as well as prayers *appearing* to have been unanswered based on our limited perspective. The sum total of these past experiences plays a role in our current level of faith in prayer.

> *Now faith is the substance of things hoped for, as it was the substance of things which have come to pass; and it is the evidence of things not seen … For it is through faith we understand that the worlds were framed by the word of God, so that the things which are seen came to be from those which are not seen.* (Hebrews 11:1–3)

As faith has substance, a substance not seen with the physical eyes, prayer has substance when backed by faith.

We often pray for things we want or need. We pray for things to happen—or not to happen. I encourage you not just to pray when you are in need, but to make connecting and conversing with God a regular part of what you do every day. Daily connection with God is an example the spiritual masters of many traditions have shown us. Prayer opens the door to God's intervention in our affairs.

Prayer is our personal conversation with God. As we discussed earlier, when we understand that God is right here, right now, everywhere, and not just in some far off remote location, it becomes quite easy to engage in conversation with our loving, ever-present Divine Parents. There is no need to try to imagine your prayers traveling up through the clouds. Your connection with God is closer than the nose on your face.

With the appropriate respect, you can pray, or talk to God, in the same way you would a dear friend. You should feel comfortable, when talking with God, to use the name for God that has the most meaning to you. You could use the name God, Father, Mother, Allah, Divine Perfection, Divine Intelligence, Infinite Intelligence, and more. God is right here. We live and have our being within God. Do you think that God, in all of God's perfection, who is the creator of all that is, would not recognize that you are talking to him/her in prayer because you are calling him/her by a specific name? God is way bigger than that. So don't worry. God will hear you! Just keep your intention clear and apply the substance of faith.

Also, please understand that it would be an error to assume that if your prayer does not immediately manifest in the *exact* way you thought it might, that you were not heard. Just have faith that God knows best *how* to answer your prayer.

> *But as for you, when you pray, enter into your inner chamber and lock the door, and pray to your Father who is in secret, and your Father who is in secret shall himself reward you openly.* (Matthew 6:6)

The phrases "inner chamber" and the "Father who is in secret" do not refer to a special room inside of any building. Instead, the "inner chamber" and "in secret" refer to the heart and soul of a person. So when we pray, we enter into the inner world, close the door to the outer world and communicate with God who is right there.

How to Pray

I am not going to provide you with a Top 10 List of Prayers to remember and recite. Instead, I'll be offering you a framework for prayer and a few examples as an illustration of this framework.

Show Gratitude

When praying, we can begin by showing gratitude. In giving thanks for those things in our lives that we are grateful for, we are in a sense sending reinforcement to God and the universe that these things—be they health, peace of mind, family, friendship, gifts, talents, our occupation or whatever—are appreciated.

Recalling what we discussed regarding the power of our thoughts, we can think of prayer as concentrated thought to the Source. Picture your prayers going directly to God. Prayer does not have to travel across the universe to reach God. We can just place our intention and trust upon knowing that God has heard our communication and prayers.

If you are asking for something in your prayer—be it health, peace of mind, forgiveness, guidance in a matter, increased faith, hope, courage, increased acceptance, abundance—strive by willing your intention to be at-one with the Higher Self. After showing sincere gratitude, you can move on the next step.

Pray for Others First

Praying for others first takes us above and outside of the "I, me, and mine" of our own little worlds and connects us with other parts of the whole in sacred unity.

Praying for others first could come in the form of prayers for healing and prayers for guidance, protection, and strength, asking that these be directed toward those who are in need. The law of giving and receiving is activated through the practice of praying for others before praying for ourselves.

> *The most efficient prayer that men can offer to a God …*
> *is helpfulness to those in need of help;*
> *for what you do for other men, the Holy One will do for you.*
> (The Aquarian Gospel of Jesus the Christ 46:17)

Some folks keep a "prayer list" of the names of those in their lives who are in need. Praying for others can go beyond any single individual, and may include communities, groups of people, or even whole nations of people.

When we view the practice of praying for others first through the light of our sacred unity with all life, we can recognize that praying for others has an effect on us, too, as we are a part of the same whole.

Pray in the Positive, Present Tense

In *The Gospel of Mark* (11:24) we read:

> *Therefore I say to you, Anything you pray for and ask, believe that you will receive it, and it will be done for you.*

We can interpret this passage as meaning that if we pray with words, yet in our heart we don't believe that the fulfillment of the prayer is possible, or that we don't deserve it, then the belief in our heart will interfere with the fulfillment of the prayer.

Always state what it is that you are asking in terms that assume that what you're asking for *has already been fulfilled.*

Here's an example of the framework of a prayer using the positive, present tense. Let's say you have a friend who is sick and you are praying for her. Your prayer could sound like:

> *Father/Mother God, I come before you to ask for and to thank you for providing healing and restoring health to my friend (name of friend). I know that it is within your power to do this in perfect ways and under grace. Nevertheless not my will, but thy will be done. Amen.*

Always hold the *outcome* you are asking for in your mind, during your prayer. Do not be concerned about the process or methodology of *how* it will happen, just have the faith that in perfect ways (which only God knows) your prayer will be fulfilled. During the prayer above, you would also hold a picture in your mind of your friend already healed and in perfect health. See the outcome for which you are asking.

Here's another example. Say that you're faced with a difficult situation in your family or your job. Your prayer may sound like:

God, thank you for providing me with the courage, strength, and wisdom to successfully resolve this issue of [state specific problem/challenge]. *I ask for your guidance and intervention in perfect ways and under grace. Nevertheless not my will, but thy will be done. Amen.*

Notice in these two examples that you are thanking God for a positive experience *as if it has already taken place.* Praying in the positive, present tense helps us to avoid praying for something to happen that we don't want to happen. We do not pray for what we don't want, we pray for positive outcomes.

Additionally, I encourage you to not use the word "want" in your prayer. If you say, "I want a better job" or "I want this pain to go away," you'll get exactly what you asked for: a state of "wanting."

A step-by-step prayer framework for effective prayer could look like this.

1. Show gratitude
2. Pray for others first
3. Pray in the positive, present tense *(state your request as if the request has already been fulfilled)*
4. Ask for the request to be made "in perfect ways and under grace"
5. Recognize that God sees a much larger *(infinite vs. finite)* view of creation and life than we do, so add: "Nevertheless not my will, but thy will be done"
6. Say, "Amen. So be it."

Types of Prayer

Some prayers are specific requests for others, such as family members, friends, coworkers, neighbors, and so on. Other prayers are for groups of people, such as those in the midst of conflicts, wars, or natural disasters. And some prayers are for nations of people. We also pray for ourselves when we are asking for God's intercession in our lives. When we listen to our hearts, we will be lead to where prayers are needed.

Remember, prayer is concentrated thought sent to the Source. Energy follows thought. Therefore, with every type of prayer we are engaged in, we are directing energy in a like manner.

The Value of Prayer

Some of the most important values of prayer are the acknowledgement that you are not separated from God and that you know you need his/her guidance and intercession on your path in life as you work toward the seven victories of the Divine Child.

God gave you independent will. With independent will, you can choose to pray or you can choose not to pray. Prayer opens the door, inviting God in to intervene in human affairs. Knowing this, you may choose to invite God in, or just to go it alone. As you work through the seven battles and seven victories, which will you choose?

It would appear that the question is an easy one to answer. So, have you yet invited God in or are you still trying to go it alone? Perhaps you've already invited God in, and do so regularly. Perhaps you haven't been direct enough or clear about inviting God in because you just weren't quite sure why or how to go about it. Hopefully, with the framework provided in this section you now feel more comfortable creating your own regular conversations with God.

In the following chapters you will be offered additional tools and guidance to support you in your journey of connection with God through the Higher Self.

The real value of prayer will be evident when you convert these words into everyday practice. Praying and having your own personal conversations with God is similar to developing a new habit. Until something new or different becomes a new habit, it requires conscious attention, remembering, and discipline.

What will you do that will enable this new habit to form?

Don't take this question lightly. In this day and age, everyone appears to be very busy. The business of life has your mind moving from one thing to another regarding family, work, finances, health issues, and relationships. Without providing yourself an answer to the question, you run the risk of prayer just amounting to a good idea you once read about. Instead, will you create a few minutes of quiet time to pray—your personal appointment with God—in the morning before the day gets started? Will you do this at the end of the day? When will it be? I encourage you to decide now and start today.

As your habit of prayer develops, you'll find that you are in conversation with God throughout the day, not just at specific times of the day. Little by little (or perhaps through grace, all at once), you'll have recognition of the Divine in your consciousness, operating in you and through you—one with you—always present.

I and my Father are of one accord. (John 10:30)

The Power of Prayer

Either you are, or will become, your own best testament to the power of prayer when you are regularly experiencing it in your own life. In your conversation and prayer with God, God will communicate with you in a virtually infinite number of ways so that you hear him. It won't be a question of *whether* God is hearing you and communicating back to you, as much as it will be a question of whether or not *you are listening.* Will you quiet the ongoing chatter of your mind long enough to listen?

The power of prayer flows stronger when we've freed ourselves of guilt and fear. Guilt and fear are blockages in the path of connecting to the Higher Self.

> *And when you stand up to pray, forgive whatever you have against any man, so that your Father in heaven will forgive you your trespasses.* (Mark 11:25)

Some people expect to hear God's reply to prayer—his side of the dialogue—to come to them in an audible, booming voice, much like might be depicted in a movie. It's my observation that God does not usually communicate in this fashion. God's response to you may come in the form of a flash of a thought, through your intuition, as an idea or an inspiration. God speaks in a soft voice that flows out of silence.

As we learn to quiet the chatter of the racing mind, we are better able to perceive God's guidance. If God is not getting through to us because of our mental chatter, he uses other ways to let us know he has heard us, such as words from a friend, lyrics to a song we hear, something we're led to read about in a book (perhaps even this book), or in a magazine or newspaper headline. The objective is to keep our eyes, ears, and most importantly, our hearts open. Remember, there is no such thing as chance. Chance is just another name for the cause and effect that are unrecognized.

When thinking about prayer, it may be helpful to view it as similar to the conversation between a child and a parent. If your child was hurting, you would want to provide comfort. If your child was in need of guidance, you would want to show your child the path to follow. If your child was asking for something that was very important to him or her, but in your experience and wisdom as a loving parent you did not believe was in your child's best interest to have, you would not comply with the request. This would not mean that you, as the parent, did not listen or hear the request. Not complying would mean you did hear the request and responded, however, your response was different than the child wanted or expected.

God knows your soul's entire history. God knows your soul's journey. God knows your soul's needs and potential. Believe that God knows best *how* to answer your prayer and rest your faith in God.

From our limited viewpoint, when we think something is in our best interest or in the best interest of someone else, we would be well served to surrender our opinion to the wisdom of God's universal viewpoint. This is why we end our prayers with, "Not my will Father, but thy will be done."

A trust built on focused communication with God is as strong as the energy, vibrations, and intention of our prayer. When we stop thinking of God as separate from us—as abiding in some far off location—we can conceive that our conversation with God is heard because God is omnipotent and omnipresent, right here, and right now. Faith means trusting that God has heard and knows best how to answer our prayers.

As we read the sacred scriptures of the Islamic faith:

Your Lord says, "Call on Me"; I will answer your prayer.
(The Qur'an 40:60)

The fact remains, you could read page after page in book after book about the power of prayer, however to *fully understand* the power of prayer you need to *experience* it. *Believe first,* practice, and then you'll experience the power for yourself.

CHAPTER 13

The Power and Purpose of Meditation

"Prayer is when you talk to God;
meditation is when you listen to God."
—Diana Robinson

M EDITATION CAN TAKE YOU into a state where you are relaxed and your mind is alert, still, and peaceful. Meditation provides physical, mental, emotional, and spiritual benefits. With confidence I can comfortably say to you that through the practice of meditation—of quieting the mind—we can build and then stand on a foundation that greatly assists us in our spiritual journey on the path to the seven victories of the Divine Child. Meditation is the science that assists us in calming our minds and claiming our divine inheritance: direct experience of oneness with God.

Meditation comes in many different forms. Let's discuss some of these now.

Meditative Activities

Some people perform meditative activities. What may be a meditative activity for one person may not be for another. Some examples of such activities are gardening, taking a walk in nature, and sewing. I am sure that you can think of a specific type of meditative activity of your own. Generally speaking, a meditative activity is one that you become totally absorbed in doing in any given moment. The activity doesn't require thinking consciously about what you're doing so your mind can rest. The lack of active mental activity is what creates the meditative state.

Whenever your mind and ego are not at the forefront of your experience you will begin to experience the *peace that passeth all understanding*. You cannot *think* about peace and stillness of the mind and achieve them. You cannot analyze them and achieve them. The moment you try to think about peace and stillness of mind or analyze them is the moment that stillness and peace vanish.

> *God's meeting place with man is in the heart, and in a still small voice he speaks; and he who hears is still.* (The Aquarian Gospel of Jesus the Christ 26:7)

Meditation

True meditation is where a person purposefully sits "in meditation." To my knowledge, taming or calming the restless, anxious, racing mind can only be accomplished one way, through the art and practice of meditation.

If you asked me, "Michael, what is the one thing I can do or learn that would have the greatest benefit, the greatest positive ripple effect in my life and on my spiritual growth?" my answer would be to learn to calm your mind through meditation.

The first two aspects to work on in meditation are controlling your breathing and stilling your mind. Our ego selves, who want to control the show in our lives, are constantly moving our minds from topic to topic, thought to thought all day long. It's true for me. Isn't this true for you? How long can you still your mind with no conscious thought before a thought pops into it as if from nowhere? Most people are surprised at how short stillness lasts when they first attempt it. Admittedly, stilling the mind's activities takes some practice. The rewards, however, are well worth the effort.

> *Those who aspire to the state of yoga* [union of the body, mind, and soul] *should seek the Self in inner solitude through meditation …. make your mind one-pointed* [on God] *in meditation, and your heart will be purified…. In the still mind, in the depths of meditation, the* [Higher] *Self reveals itself…. Abiding joy comes to those who still the mind. Freeing themselves from the taint of self-will, with their consciousness unified, they become one with Brahman* [God]. (Bhagavad Gita 6:10–27)

For the Higher Self, the Christ consciousness connecting you with God, to be recognized and be heard, you must first be able to quiet your mind.

> *Be still and know that I am God.* (Psalm 46:10)

There are many styles, objectives, and levels of meditation practice. Many books can be found that teach these variations on meditation. In my opinion, learning a proven method and process for meditation in a class is better than reading about it. This particular chapter therefore is not dedicated to meditation instruction. The point here is rather to shine a light on the importance of meditation, and explain what I feel should be its primary goals: first, seeking to slow down and quiet the racing, random, reactive thoughts of the mind; and next, moving into personal realization of oneness with God.

In my experience, when you start meditating for twenty to thirty minutes each day you will notice and feel a difference in your state of mind after the first month! Countless material and spiritual benefits will come into your life once you are able to slow down and still your racing mind. For now, allow me to elaborate on just one benefit. This benefit applies to every one of us and aids us in our travels through life and through the seven victories of the Divine Child.

In any given week, countless events take place in our lives: thoughts, conversations, interactions, and what we observe, read, or watch on TV. Just for a moment, let us call these events *stimuli*. To every stimulus, we provide a particular response. Our responses come in the form of thoughts, words spoken, or actions taken in relation to the stimulus. The untamed mind will immediately jump from the stimulus to the response reactively. In fact, reaction to a stimulus may happen so fast that we even find it difficult to discern the response from the stimulus. Reactions automatically flow out of past mental scripts (our current mental map) and habits.

However, the calm mind, one that was achieved through the practice of meditation, experiencing the same event or stimulus is less apt to simply react. Instead, the calm-minded person "pauses" between a stimulus and a response. In the space that is created by the pause before the response, the person can sort through the situation and experience a sense of freedom to choose consciously how (and even if) he or she will respond.

So many of our life experiences flow out of, and are a function of our current perspective. The freedom and peace that the tamed or calmed mind provides us allow us the opportunity to see things differently: to gain a larger, deeper perspective of a situation to which we might otherwise have been blind. This is just one of many, many benefits that come our way through the practice of meditation.

Additionally, through your own meditations you'll find out that you will:

- Be calmer (reduce tension, uneasiness, and fear).
- Be able to better handle stress and stressful situations (become less reactive).
- Reduce and transmute negative emotions.
- Increase your focus and concentration.
- Have an increased sense of peace and awareness.
- Experience an overall increased sense of well-being.
- Recognize your oneness with God and become more attuned in your relationship with God.

As your experience with meditation and your focused discipline in your meditations advances, your consciousness will expand and you'll become more aware of the non-physical realities of the subtle energy bodies that surround you. You will become aware of the Higher Self, and move forward in your awareness of your oneness with God.

When meditation is mastered, the mind is unwavering like a flame of a lamp in a windless place. (The Bhagavad Gita 6:19)

CHAPTER 14
Self-mastery

*"Above all the grace and the gifts that Christ gives
to his beloved is that of overcoming self."*
—Saint Francis of Assisi

SELF-MASTERY BEGINS WITH self-awareness, which means being conscious of what we are thinking and feeling at any given moment. Through self-awareness, we can consciously choose our thoughts, words, and actions—not operate our lives out of reactivity and habit. We can consciously choose our perspective and how we view life's ebbs and flows.

Self-mastery requires conscious discipline; it raises us above being the actor in our lives. It lifts us to the perspective of a director watching a play unfold.

Self-mastery moves us beyond being a puppet on the strings of life, pulling and pushing us, to a state of being the puppeteer, moving in divine harmony. Self-mastery allows us to claim what is rightly ours: liberation from the bondage of limitation. Self-mastery is a way of stepping out of the outward appearances of the world in order to reconnect with divine will.

Self-mastery is a process of reclaiming all that has always been yours: your oneness with God. It helps you conquer the duality of the material world and lower vibrations this world has offered up to you as a way of experiencing the Higher Attributes.

Self-mastery is the ability to be aware of our thoughts and feelings and to transmute them, to change our state of mind and being, in an instant, at will. When we change our state of mind, we change our energy. Being able to will peace and acceptance, for example, can transmute conflicted thoughts and feelings in an instant. This reminds me of the passage from *The Gospel of John* (3:3) where Jesus is teaching Nicodemus. He says:

> *Truly, truly, I say to you, If a man is not born again, he cannot see the kingdom of God.*

"Born again" means to change our thoughts and habits.

Why Is Self-Mastery Important?

In the first chapter of *The Book of Genesis* (1:27–28) we read:

> *So God created man in his own image, in the image of God he created him; male and female he created them. And God blessed them, and God said to them, be fruitful, and multiply, and fill the earth, and subdue it.*

Now we could talk about the "be fruitful" part of the passage, or about the "multiply" part of the passage, but what do we make of the "subdue it" part? What is meant by "fill the earth, and subdue it?"

Random House Unabridged Dictionary defines the verb "subdue" as to "overcome" and to "tame." We could understand this passage to mean God wants us to learn to overcome the material world (by rising above the obvious outward appearance of things) and tame the mind. We live in a world of duality, a world where opposites exist, we have love and fear, we have faith and doubt, we have selflessness and selfishness, we have forgiveness and also guilt and resentment. By their very nature, all pairs of opposites can create—or appear to create—challenges in our lives. By calming or taming the mind through meditation, we can begin to proactively change our thoughts from one end of duality into its opposite. We will discuss this process in more detail in the following chapters. Simply put, once learned, this part of self-mastery can change your life!

All sacred scriptures ultimately are teaching self-mastery. They are showing us how to apply the steps in our lives that enable us to overcome challenges, steps that lift us up to the level of our true nature as God's Divine Child. I share the steps towards self-mastery with you, confident in the knowledge that as you take each step, each day, and as I do, together we are embracing a new, more expanded perspective and creating opportunities to be ever-clearer reflections of who we really are.

The Five Steps toward Self-mastery

The steps of self-mastery are:

1. Calming the racing, anxious, reactive mind.
2. Viewing life experiences through an eternal lens (a view broader than one physical birth and death).
3. Understanding and applying spiritual laws.
4. Making the Higher Attributes the mental map through which we filter our life experiences.
5. Accepting the truth that you are God's child and strive to be an ever-clearer reflection of this truth.

Now, let us examine each of these five steps in detail.

Step 1: Calming the Racing, Anxious, Reactive Mind

Many people are hostage to the untamed mind. The untamed mind is constantly in motion, racing from topic to topic. The untamed or unsubdued mind is engaged, for the most part, in replaying past events, tugging at people to relive the past *or* projecting fear of the unknown future. The very nature of this type of mind is anxious. The level of anxiety can range from a small amount of nervous tension to a large amount of anxiety. Any level of anxiety can cause undue stress, fear, and unhappiness.

You may be wondering, *Well my mind is restless and turbulent, but it has always been this way.* Try to train it. It may be true that a restless mind takes some effort to control; trying to control the mind may feel like trying to tame the wind. However, each of us has the will power to tame the mind. Remember, you are in charge of your mind; your mind is not in charge of you!

Think about this. If you aren't controlling your mind, who is? The truth is that your mind and your thoughts are the only things you really have any control over.

So how does one go about this aspect of self-mastery: taming the mind? To my knowledge, taming or calming the restless, anxious, racing mind can only be accomplished one way: through the art and practice of meditation. How many times have you heard or read about the benefits of meditation? Since we've already discussed some of the benefits of meditation, I won't repeat myself here. Taming the racing, reactive mind through meditation is the first step towards self-mastery.

Step 2: View Life's Experiences Through an Eternal Lens

Viewing life through an eternal lens allows us to view our life experiences in a much broader sense than one physical birth and physical death. God is the God of the living, not of the dead. Life continues on after the change called "death." Viewing our life experiences through a lens of a single lifetime is equivalent to trying to see life through a peephole in a door: We only can see a very narrow perspective of the big picture. Seeing life and our life experiences through an eternal lens or viewpoint, on the other hand, allows us to have an expanded perspective of our lives today.

Of course, the finite mind cannot fully comprehend the eternal. We use the terminology "eternal lens" as a description to help us expand our perspective and look beyond the brief period of one lifetime. For a lifetime of 100 years is still only a speck of time when placed on an eternal timeline. As we have agreed, we are spiritual beings, having a human experience. Spiritual beings, whether in or out of a physical body, are alive within God's presence, which by its very nature is eternal.

As we view life experiences through an eternal lens, step by step we begin to perceive events in our lives and the world around us quite differently. Not only do we become less reactive to life, but we can begin to make sense of things that previously we could not understand or reconcile from our former perspective.

Step 3: Understanding and Applying Spiritual Laws

Having a working understanding of spiritual laws can assist us in our daily lives and provide us with a level of perspective that helps to remove some of the mystery from why certain things happen to us in life. Having an understanding of spiritual laws acts as our navigational system as we journey along the path to the victories of the Divine Child.

In *The Book of Exodus* from the Old Testament, it is written that God gave Moses the Ten Commandments. These commandments were largely stated from the perspective of "Thou shall not." In the New Testament, it is written that Master Jesus gave us a new commandment, a spiritual law, which is stated differently. This law is at the root of all the other spiritual laws.

Jesus said to them, Love the Lord God with all your heart and all your soul and with all your might and with all your mind. This is the greatest and the first commandment. And the second is like to it, Love your neighbor as yourself. On these two commandments hang the law and the prophets.
(Matthew 22:37–40)

The main message of the gospels and spiritual laws is, in one word, love. The law of love is the active cohesive element and essence of God in all creation. God's love is the first cause and origination of creation, which manifests as the light and life that are reflected through the indwelling Universal Divine Child, the Higher Self. In the passage above, Master Jesus is telling us to live in harmony with the vibration of love, to embrace the love-based thought system.

The law of love is at the core of the Higher Attributes. You could say that it is like the root system and trunk of a tree, and other Higher Attributes are like the branches of the tree. The leaves of the tree are our own thoughts, words, and actions, which are manifestations of the nature of the branches, trunk, and roots of the tree.

Since the law of love is God's energy—although changeless and eternal—it is in constant motion, constantly flowing. When in error we create energy through our thoughts, words, or actions that is in disharmony with the law of love energy, *we create* a state of energetic imbalance and our lives go awry.

When we create energy—through our thoughts, words or actions—which is not in harmony with love, the law of cause and effect works to rebalance the energy we created in error. This rebalancing of energy, by its nature, produces the effects we see in our lives. These effects need not be viewed as punishment or retribution from an angry God. The effects that occur stem from causes we ourselves have set in motion yesterday, last month, last year, and even in prior lifetimes. This is what is meant by the statement *"For whatever a man sows, that shall he also reap."* (Galatians 6:7). Having this as a frame of reference will assist you, especially when applying Step 2: viewing life's experiences through an eternal lens—a view broader than one physical birth and death.

When we combine seeing life through an eternal lens with a working knowledge of the spiritual laws, we understand that all things, including thoughts, are made up of energy, and there is a rhythm to the energy. The ebbs and flows of energy will, without fail, seek to be in balance. Seeing through the eternal lens teaches us that we may experience or observe particular effects in our lives—say a sickness or hurt of some kind—and can be assured that energy and life are only seeking balance, not to punish us.

There's an old saying, "It does not matter *what* happens to me; instead, *how I respond* to what happens to me that matters most." How we respond to the effects in our lives is, in large part, a function of how we view or perceive this larger picture.

Know this. Our current state is always a result of our past choices. It is wise to understand this, but there is no value in judging yourself because of it. It is what it is. The past is past. Instead, choose to place your conscious awareness on the present and on embodying the Higher Attributes. For it is the current seeds we plant today through our thoughts, words, and actions that will create our tomorrows. With this knowledge and awareness, we can become conscious co-creators.

Step 4: Making the Higher Attributes the Mental Map Through Which We Filter Our Life Experiences

I have made reference to the Higher Attributes on several occasions. Since we will be covering them in detail in chapters 17–23, I'll just list a few of them here so that you have some context to refer to as we look at how we can use the Higher Attributes as a mental map to filter our life experiences.

Higher Attribute	Lower Attribute
Self-control/Discipline	Wrong use of energy
Hope	Despair
Forgiveness	Guilt/Resentment
Selfless service	Selfishness
Love	Fear/Hatred
Compassion/Mercy	Indiscriminate judgment
Faith	Doubt
Courage	Helplessness
Humility	Pride/arrogance
Truth/Continuity of life	Death
Abundance	Scarcity
Wisdom/Understanding	Narrow-mindedness

We all have free will: meaning, we have the freedom to choose which end of the Attribute Ladder we create and live our lives from each day. Will it be from the Higher Attribute side of the chart above or from the Lower Attribute side?

Unless we are aware and therefore consciously choose to live each day from the perspective of a Higher Attribute, we risk (depending on the circumstance and our past habits and conditioning) bouncing back and forth between the Lower Attributes and the Higher Attributes.

Earlier, we talked about beliefs and how we form our current mental maps. All of our experiences and interactions flow through the filter of our mental map. The goal of Step 4 in self-mastery is to make the Higher Attributes the foundation of our mental map.

Part of self-mastery is becoming sufficiently self-aware to gauge if we are filtering, or processing, life through any of the Lower Attributes. And, if so, to become capable of calling upon and allowing the Higher Self to guide us in transforming our thoughts, words, and actions so that they flow from the Higher Self.

In Step 1, we talked about calming the racing mind. Being able to slow down the mind and insert a "pause" between stimulus and our response we allow ourselves time to make conscious choices rather than reacting out of habit or emotional impulsiveness. Now tying Step 1 and Step 4 together, you can see that a person can choose—in the space created by the pause—to filter or think about any situation at hand through the perspective of these Higher Attributes.

Step 5: Accept the Truth that You Are God's Child and Strive to Be an Ever-Clearer Reflection of this Truth

In actuality, this step has two components.

1. Accept the truth that you are one of God's children
2. Strive to be an ever-clearer reflection of this truth

What gets in our way of accepting the truth that each of us is God's Divine Child? Is it because we perceive (through our own limited perspective and judgment) that we are not perfect in every way today? Is it that we think we are not worthy to be called a child of God? Is it that somewhere along the line you heard or were told that God had only one son (and you aren't him)? At the core of our being, who are we if not sons and daughters of God?

Did you know that nowhere in the gospels of the New Testament would you find *Jesus saying* that he is the only son of God? Furthermore, in *The Gospel of Thomas*, which is a non-canonical collection of sayings from Master Jesus, you will read the following statement quite to the contrary:

> *Jesus said, If those who lead you say to you, See, the kingdom is in the sky, then the birds of the sky will precede you. Rather the kingdom is inside of you, and it is outside of you. When you come to know yourselves, then you will become*

known, and you will realize that it is you who are sons of the living father. (The Gospel of Thomas, saying 3)

And:

Jesus said to her, Do not come near me; for I have not yet ascended to my Father; but go to my brethren and say to them, I am ascending to my Father and your Father, and my God and your God. (John 20:17)

The fact is, we could quote scriptures all day referencing each of us as children of God, but until we come to realize this truth for ourselves, the scriptures are just words. Individually, each of us must nourish and provide the necessary environment for the seeds of recognition and realization to grow towards knowing that we are God's children. I am here to simply plant a seed of reminder in your mind, and offer some fertile ground for this seed to grow.

The realization that we are *all* sons and daughters of God is what Master Jesus spoke about when he said:

Call no one on earth father, for one is your Father in heaven.
(Matthew 23:9)

What does the realization of the second part of Step 5, striving to be an ever-clearer reflection of this truth, really mean? Just for a moment, imagine this. Imagine that you had a dream—one of those very vivid dreams that feels so real. In this dream, the cloudiness surrounding your awareness lifted away. And in this state of clear awareness, you were shown and came to know who you really were. You could feel in the depth of your being, in the very depth of your soul, that you are a child of God. Beyond intellect and beyond feeling, you just knew that you knew. Then you awakened with full awareness of what you had experienced in the clarity of your dream. You felt light, at ease, and at peace. You then went about your day viewing life and filtering your experiences from the new, awakened state of awareness. Wouldn't that have been great?

Embrace this awareness. Holding it in mind, ask yourself these questions:

- How does my new awareness affect my *thoughts* throughout the day?
- How does my new awareness affect the *words* I speak throughout the day?
- How does my new awareness affect my *actions* throughout the day?

I would conclude that it is natural for us to live through the day from the perspective of the Higher Attributes. In times that we slip, and perhaps are not as clear of a reflection of our true selves as we could be, we do not need to be angry or feel guilty. As self-mastered people, we can adjust or correct ourselves, if need be, bringing ourselves back into alignment with the Higher Attributes. This is self-transformation in action.

I can assure you that no matter how light or how heavy life's burdens feel for you at this moment, through the application of these five steps of self-mastery, you can experience firsthand, and in a very personal way, God's peace, love, and guidance in your life from now on.

In the *Illustrated Book of Sacred Scriptures* (Quest Books, 1998), Timothy Freke provides a description of the qualities and behaviors of people who have attained self-mastery. It is a description each of us can relate to, and work to accomplish one step at a time. Let's consider how Timothy Freke describes these qualities and behaviors:

> *They transcend their personal selves and discover the Universal Self. They follow God's will. They accept whatever happens. They have no personal agenda, so they know*

neither failure nor success. They see others as a part of God and so are nonjudgmental and compassionate. They witness the omnipresent evolution of consciousness and therefore do not see good and evil, but only a continual striving from ignorance to knowledge. They are temporary residents of earth, like the rest of us. Yet they do not believe they are only a mortal body and personality, but know themselves to be the eternal consciousness, which inhabits it. They are individuals, but not separate from God.

Applying these transformative steps of self-mastery in our everyday lives points us in the direction of becoming ever-clearer reflections of who we are: sons and daughters of God.

If I change my mind, I can change my choices; if I change my choices, I can change my outcome ... that is, I can change my life

PART FIVE

The Battles and Victories of the Divine Child

"Out of compassion I destroy the darkness of their ignorance. From within them I light the lamp of wisdom and dispel all darkness from their lives."

—The Bhagavad Gita 10:11

CHAPTER 15
The Raging War within

"Saints and sages, thinkers and philosophers, priests and scientific inquirers have tried for centuries to understand the enigmatic nature of the human soul. They find man a paradoxical being; one capable of descent into the darkest abysses of evil, and yet equally capable of ascent to the sublimest heights of nobility. They discover two creatures within his breast—one related to the demons and the other related to the angels."
—Paul Brunton, *The Secret Path*

THE BATTLE BETWEEN THE Lower Self and the Higher Self is an internal battle, fought every day in the minds and hearts of all men and women. The challenges that these internal battles create in our lives exist regardless of our beliefs, religion, culture, or race. This battle is taking place, to a greater or lesser extent, whether we are conscious of it or not.

The battle between the Lower Self and the Higher Self has been in the consciousness of humanity for millennia. How many scriptures, books, stories, and movies have been written, read, and viewed based on the basic storyline of Good vs. Evil? We see the battle of Light vs. Darkness all around us. We even see it represented in cartoons where a character faced with a decision is depicted with a little angel on one shoulder and a little devil on the other. The little angel and little devil argue their different points of view on the situation into the ears of the cartoon character. Ultimately, the character has to make a decision based on this symbolic *internal dialogue.*

This is not terribly different than situations we might find ourselves dealing with in our own lives. As we become aware that an inner battle is taking place, we can proceed daily, even moment to moment, to embrace the perspective that if we recognize the battles and make conscious choices—led by the Higher Self—we will eventually ensure the victory.

The term "battle" might seem too grand, too substantial at times. The term "internal conflict" might seem to fit some situations more appropriately. It doesn't matter what we call it, make no mistake, many times throughout a given week, even every day, we are choosing between the Lower Attributes of the Lower Self (ego) and the Higher Attributes of the Higher Self in our thoughts, words, and actions.

In many cases, we need to consciously transmute our thoughts, words, and actions from a Lower Attribute to a Higher Attribute. This is where self-mastery comes in. When we change the polarity of our thoughts, words, and actions, we are purposefully changing our energy, focus, and perspective.

We typically experience many mini-victories along the way whenever we transmute a Lower Attribute into a Higher Attribute. As we experience more and more of these mini-victories, we are in a process of replacing old, and no longer useful patterns of thinking, speaking, and acting from the fear-based thought system with new patterns from the love-based thought system that are more in harmony with the Higher Self within.

These battles must be experienced. You can say we chose the battles for ourselves to experience. We need not try to run from or avoid these battles. They are guiding us along the path to why we are here: to experience the Higher Attributes and ultimately to experience oneness with God. Even though some of the situations we face in life can be quite painful when we're in the midst of them, as is the case of an illness, accident, grief at the death of a loved one, divorce, or an abusive situation, to name only a few, these, or similar challenges in life give us opportunities to engage in the seven victories of the Divine Child.

We can choose to embrace the *opportunities* that our life challenges and other experiences provide to us. Our lives allow us the opportunity to *experience* the Higher Attributes and become, day by day, ever clearer reflections of who we really are: sons and daughters of God.

> *And the Spirit bears witness to our spirit, that we are the children of God.* (Romans 8:16)

CHAPTER 16

Seven Battles and Seven Victories

"When your mind has overcome the confusion of duality, you will attain the state of holy indifference to things you hear and things you have heard."
—The Bhagavad Gita 2:52

EACH OF THE NEXT seven chapters is an exploration of one of the seven battles and seven victories of the Divine Child. As we explore each one, we'll review the common challenges that people face in varying degrees. You'll learn steps you can take and tools you can use during each battle that will assist you in achieving your ultimate victory. I encourage you to keep in mind how you can integrate the Universal Wisdom Tools we discussed in Part Four into your process of transmuting the Lower Attributes into Higher Attributes, as these will assist you greatly in being victorious and claiming your divine inheritance.

As you are reading about, learning about, and, in some cases, remembering past experiences of these battles, do your best to be aware of how you're feeling in regard to each one. Stay in touch with what is going on inside: You may experience many different types of thoughts and feelings. Don't judge your thoughts and feelings, just observe them. As you progress through each of the seven chapters notice if your observations about the battle fall into one of the following three categories:

Category A. You feel that this battle is an easy one for you to win, and in many ways you've already experienced victory over this battle.

Category B. You feel that you're currently in the midst of this particular battle; the battle is in progress in your life.

Category C. You feel like this battle is so large that you wonder how you're ever going to be able to win it and experience victory.

It will be helpful, as you read through the seven chapters, to pause and reflect on how your life relates to the description of the battle/victory. Come back to this page when you're done reading the chapter. Still your mind, apply your intuition, and then—using the chart below—write an A, B, or C in the margin next to the number of the battle/victory that you just read about. Choose the letter that you honestly feel best describes which category you are in relative to that battle. Use the chart provided to record your impressions.

	A	B	C
Victory #1			
Victory #2			
Victory #3			
Victory #4			
Victory #5			
Victory #6			
Victory #7			

When you have completed Part Five, you'll know exactly which of the three categories you're in regarding each of the seven battles/ victories. In all likelihood, you're in mixed stages, as most people are. For example, for battle/victory #1, #3, and #4, you could be in Category A. For battle/victory #2 and #5, you could be in Category B. For battle/victory #6 and #7, you could be in Category C. The chart allows you to see your answers as a snapshot.

Do not judge yourself based on your sorting. This is for your benefit only. The process is a dynamic one, and it may be helpful to return to it at a later date to reevaluate your progress. Remember, this will be valuable information for you to refer back to at a future date. Please do not skip this exercise!

When we are aware that they are taking place, the battles forge us along a path of experiences that, if we make proper adjustments in our thought system, can lead us to self-mastery. Experiencing these victories is the path of the Divine Child and prepares us to claim our divine inheritance.

Who Are These Battles Against?

Becoming conscious of the battle of light vs. darkness is a giant step forward in life. It is not uncommon to believe that the Higher Attributes come from within and the Lower Attributes come from an outside source. In truth, both come from within us.

Although it seems natural to look outside to identify who or what we are battling against, looking outside is the work of the ego, a trick of misdirection. Don't be fooled for a moment and think that your battle is against some force or another person. These battles are internal battles. Oh yes, there will be other people involved in situations in our lives who appear, on the surface, to be causing our frustration, hurt, or pain. Don't trick yourself in believing that your issues are with such people. Others are simply acting as instruments for us to learn and remember the Divine Child within. Every situation we face in our lives that challenges us facilitates us in transmuting Lower Attributes into their opposite Higher Attributes.

Once your awareness increases to the point where you understand the characteristics of the Lower Self and the Higher Self and can recognize when the battles are occurring, you can apply the knowledge you now have of the power of thought and creative energy, the power of prayer, the art of meditation, and the steps of self-mastery to win them.

In and of themselves, there is nothing difficult about embodying Higher Attributes or incorporating them into your thought system and into your life. They will flow naturally out of you, if and when you allow them, for you have divinity in you by nature. If you are struggling and find a particular Higher Attribute more challenging, examine your beliefs. You were either taught or decided at some point in the past to believe in the idea it would be difficult.

Every battle is a process of moving through the challenges towards the Higher Attributes. Just remember that these battles are internal. They only exist inside of you. They do not exist outside of the mind of the individual experiencing them. The process of transmuting the Lower Self into at-onement with the Higher Self will reveal this fact to you. This is a process of cultivating the Higher Attributes within yourself and making them your own. A sure sign that you are winning the battle is when the Higher Attributes become dominant in your everyday life. As the battles fall away, the environment in which they take place changes. Victory is now yours.

The Principle of Polarity

Before leaving off and beginning our study of the seven battles of the Divine Child, let me introduce you to a concept that you may find useful in becoming victorious. It goes back to antiquity and was originated by Hermes Trismegistus (a blending of the Egyptian god Thoth and the Greek god Hermes), whose adherents defined seven spiritual principles currently recorded in *The Kybalion*, one of which is the *principle of polarity.*

The principle of polarity states that everything that exists has an opposite, and can only be known by comparison with the opposite. Philosophically this concept makes sense considering the nature of duality in our world. We cannot understand joy without understanding sorrow. We cannot know light without understanding darkness. Opposites are two sides of the same coin that always are defined by experience of the opposite.

In working with this principle it is useful to understand that between two polarities, two opposites, such as a Lower Attribute and its corresponding Higher Attribute, we will often find ourselves experiencing various degrees as we move from one to the other. The extremes exist along the same pole, which includes gradations in between.

To illustrate this concept, think of it in terms of light and darkness, which are polar opposites. At one end of the pole is very bright light; at the other end, pitch-black darkness. As you move from the darkness toward the light, often you don't just go from one to the other, as you would by flipping a light switch on. Rather you experience a kind of dawning of light, like daybreak. You move from deep darkness, to slightly less darkness, to somewhere in the middle between light and dark where they are about equal, to increasing brightness, then to more lightness, until you reach bright light. The movement from one end of the pole to the opposite end was essentially a change in rate of vibration, from darkness (slower vibration) into light (faster vibration).

So what does this have to do with the seven battles of the Divine Child? A lot. Because we understand that all things are created mentally before they manifest in the physical world, we know that we can move toward the Higher Attributes by changing the polarity of our own thoughts, and we also know that this is likely to happen in degrees. *We can immediately move ourselves from a Lower-attribute state, into a Higher-attribute state, simply by changing the focus of our thoughts, like turning on a light switch.* But we also can embrace our mini-victories as we bring increased light into our darkness until we reach the full brightness of the Higher Attribute shining in our lives.

Specifically, if you find that your thoughts are at a lower, opposite end of the pole of a given Higher Attribute, acknowledge this fact and then change your thoughts to those consistent with the Higher Attribute. Consciously redirect your thoughts using focus, will power, and discipline. Your energy will follow your thoughts if you are diligent.

This is not to suggest that you should deny your feelings. It is best to acknowledge the feelings you are experiencing, and then choose to experience the Higher Attribute that is a clearer reflection of who you really are. Applying the principle of polarity in a dualistic world is to know and experience the Higher Attributes *by* knowing and experiencing their opposites. With every *mini-victory* over the Lower Self and a Lower Attribute, you will gain strength. In fact, you'll find that your strength, wisdom, and the insights you need to overcome various life challenges continue to grow and grow.

You see, your soul already knows the Higher Attributes. It knows goodness. It knows love and selflessness. It knows faith and forgiveness. It knows compassion and mercy. But it *seeks to experience what it knows*. Because of the principle of polarity, the only way for the soul to really know what it knows is to experience the opposite.

> *All things are twofold, one opposite the other, and he has made nothing incomplete. One confirms the good things of the other.* (Sirach 42:24–25)

As we move forward into the seven victories of the Divine Child, I envision each attribute as a ladder, with the Lower Attribute at the bottom of the ladder and the Higher Attribute at the top of the ladder. I liken the movement that we make when we move ourselves from a Lower Attribute up to a Higher Attribute similar to climbing up the rungs of a ladder. Therefore, when I use the term *Attribute Ladder*, I am making reference to the process of climbing from a Lower Attribute up to a Higher Attribute.

CHAPTER 17

Victory #1
Joy

"Happiness is when what you think, what you say, and what you do are in harmony."
—Mahatma Gandhi

Higher Attributes

Discipline/Self-control
Hope
Purity of heart

Lower Attributes

Misdirected use of energy
Discouragement/Despair
Impurity

APPLY THE PRINCIPLE OF polarity to move up the ladder of each attribute. To change your vibration and polarity from Lower Attributes into the Higher Attributes, *immediately change the focus of your thoughts.*

The battleground of joy is any situation in which we face a push and pull between: discipline/self-control and a misdirected use of energy, hope and discouragement/despair, and purity of heart and impurity. Let's look at each type of battleground in turn.

Discipline/Self-control vs. Misdirected Use of Energy

Without a doubt, it will require applying varying degrees of discipline as you work through the seven battles and seven victories. Some battles may require mental discipline, while others may require emotional or physical discipline to experience your victories.

As a reminder, there will be times that a given battle may *appear* to be going on *outside* of you—do not get tricked into believing this for one minute—make no mistake, these battles are personal and are going on *inside* of you. Often times outside events, or other people in your life, surface and act as a trigger or catalyst causing you to face and work on these private battles.

I was taught that the definition of discipline was "doing" the right things—meaning, certain behaviors—especially when no one else was looking. While there appears to be some truth in this statement, this definition is incomplete because there are events that precede all "doing," "action," and "behavior." Our thoughts *(both what and how we think)* precede our actions. Our beliefs, or mental maps, influence and provide direction to our thoughts, whether or not we are conscious of how this happens.

So where do discipline and self-control fit into the picture of joy? If we want to be inwardly harmonious, it is important to develop the discipline to no longer *react* to events in our lives. We must be able to examine our emotions, especially the ones that could be labeled as "destructive," which are often associated with a Lower Attribute. Developing discipline and self-control is a process of learning how to manage your thoughts and emotions so that they won't control you. Having the discipline to pause and become aware of your own thoughts and the self-control to suspend them the very moment you are faced with challenges is invaluable. If you do not habitually react to life and life's circumstances, but instead, consciously choose what you think, say, and do, your life will become more joyful.

Reactive thoughts come from beliefs developed through years of programming by the influence of others, as well as through our own observations and experiences. Living life *reactively*, by default and not by choice, is a misdirected use of energy when our habitual thoughts, words, and actions are reflections of any of the Lower Attributes.

Daily, we are faced with making a multitude of decisions about how we will use our energy to respond to life. The question is, will we use our energy to move up a rung on the Attribute Ladder, and express the will of the Higher Self, or will we use our energy to stay at a lower rung and reinforce the will of the Lower Self? The exciting thing is that moment by moment we get to choose. Now, that's empowerment!

> *Let this mind be in you, which was also in Christ Jesus.* (Philippians 2:5)

The mind referred to in the quote above is none other than the Universal Divine Child, the Higher Self.

> *The supreme Reality stands revealed in the consciousness of those who have conquered themselves.* (The Bhagavad Gita 6:7)

Hope vs. Discouragement/Despair

To have hope is to believe and trust. Sounds a lot like faith, doesn't it?

> *Now Faith is the substance of things hoped for, as it was the substance of things which have come to pass; and it is the evidence of things not seen.* (Hebrews 11:1)

Any situation in which there is discouragement is an emotional battle. If left unchecked by our will to control and direct our own thoughts, this type of battle can evolve into a mental battle as well. Sometimes people experience discouragement because they've been hopeful about something that runs counter to the spiritual laws. When the result of what was hoped for does not *appear* to turn out as people planned or expected, discouragement often sets in. That's when they must change their focus.

Discouragement and despair come about from a state of mind where our focus is fixed on problems. When the mind recycles problems and issues, it's not easy to see a clear way out. We find ourselves in a proverbial pit where we cannot see the light of day. A change in focus enables us to direct and allow the mind to use our energy toward creating solutions, as opposed to despairing about our problems.

We can change our state of mind by changing our perception of what is *causing* the discouragement. Both discouragement and lack of hope come from mentally replaying past events or projecting made-up scenarios into the future. When we pull ourselves back into the present moment, both begin to fade away. Based on the nature and degree of the issue or issues we're facing, changing our point of view may come effortlessly once we decide to do it or it may require the discipline of repeated, focused effort.

The mind is a goal-seeking device. By asking ourselves a new set of questions in any situation, the mind can be encouraged to refocus its power on solutions. As we do this, discouragement and despair are transmuted into hope.

In certain situations people may need and benefit from the help of another to assist them in being able to see things differently before they can adjust their own thoughts to be in harmony with God's will. This assistance can come from a good friend, a parent, a therapist, or a spiritual counselor.

Taking the higher path, as embodied in the statement, "*Father, not my will, but thy will be done*," allows us to turn anything we're *hoping for* over to God. As we turn our issues over to God to solve "in perfect ways and under grace," we invoke the presence and eternal power of our Divine Parents to intercede in our lives. Through divine harmony, we know that all will be as it should be. How could it be any other way?

We can also experience hope by helping others find hope. So remember to provide hope to those who are in need of uplifting. *We receive only that which we give away.* When we can give hope to others, we open the door to receive the same. Giving hope to others can be done in many ways: A kind word, a poem, an article, or a book could provide the needed words at just the right time to instill hope in others.

Purity of Heart vs. Impurity

When we speak of purity, we are speaking about purity of the heart and the intentions of the individual. As we read in *Proverbs* 23:7:

> *As a man thinketh in his heart, so he is.*

If an individual is functioning at the lower end of the Purity/Impurity Attribute Ladder, the individual will manifest all sorts of lies, deceit, and corruption, and attempt to inflict harm on his or her fellow brothers and sisters. The individual's heart is hardened by the disharmony and pain caused by being misaligned with the Higher Self.

> *Create in me a clean heart, O God, and renew a right spirit within me.* (Psalm 51:10)

Don't be fooled into thinking that you can hide your true intentions. Your intentions are recorded in your subconscious mind. Similarly, we do not really know the true intentions of another person. Consider this saying I once heard, "We judge ourselves by our intentions and we judge others by their behaviors." The behaviors of another person are observable, while his or her intentions are not. Admittedly, sometimes a person's outward behaviors are incongruent with his or her inner intentions. Having said that, we are not in a position to *judge* another person's intentions. How could we? It's easy to find fault in another person, and more difficult to see our own. The faster we can let go of the need to filter others people's behaviors through our own experiences and opinions, our own mental map, the faster we will find peace and joy enter into our lives.

We were all children at one time. That's why it's such a pleasure to watch children play; it reminds us of our own natural joy and wonder. We can perceive joy on their faces, we can hear it in their laughter, and we can see the wonder in their eyes. Children are great examples for us of how to live in the present moment. Don't children have pure hearts and motive in their sheer innocence? Even to the hardened heart, seeing a baby touches the soul. Strive to become pure of heart like a little child.

Do not torment over past errors—we've all made them. Today is a new day filled with opportunity and options, a chance to make new choices and gain a new awareness of who you really are. Strive daily to live life in accord with the Higher Attributes.

Moving up this Attribute Ladder means acting from pure motives. To remember, or better yet, to possess the daily awareness that not only were you created in the image and likeness of God, but that you, dear soul, are a son or daughter of God, will help you climb these rungs. As you remember who you really are as a part of God, you'll allow an increased amount of light and love to enter and flow through you. A pure heart will be reflected in daily thoughts, words, and actions that are pure.

Do your best to act with pure motive, desiring only to manifest the Higher Attributes while you are here in a physical body on the vibrational plane of matter and your life will become more joyful.

> *Whatever is true, whatever is honest, whatever is just, whatever is pure, whatever is lovely, whatever is of good report; if there is any virtue, think on these things.* (Philippians 4:8)

Prayers

Use the following prayers to assist you in winning your battle of joy.

A Prayer for Discipline/Self-control

Dear Heavenly Father, thank you for helping me find the discipline and self-control to pause and reflect, not just to respond and react to life's challenges. I'm aware that all *perceived* challenges that cross my path are opportunities for self-mastery through discipline and self-control. Discipline and self-control enter into my being in perfect ways and under grace. Amen.

A Prayer for Hope

I call on you, my Divine Parents, to intercede into my life now. I am open to you. Surround me with the energy of hope, and dispel from my being any thoughts and emotions of despair. I no longer accept thoughts and feelings of despair, as they are not clear reflections of my true Self. I know that on the other side of hope is faith, and on the other side of faith is knowing. I know that within your hands, Father/ Mother, divine harmony is now restored into my life and all is as it should be. Set my mind and my feet squarely in the light of your path in perfect ways and under grace. Amen.

A Prayer for Purity of Heart

Divine Mother, I no longer react to life out of habit or past conditioning. Through the light of your presence, renew a pure heart in me, in perfect ways and under grace. From this day forward, I think, speak, and act from a place of awareness that all people are your divine children and my spiritual brothers and sisters. Amen.

CHAPTER 18

Victory #2
Freedom

"Freedom is oxygen of the soul."
—Moshe Dayan

Higher Attributes

Freedom
Forgiveness
Justice

Lower Attributes

Limitation
Guilt/Resentment
Injustice

APPLY THE PRINCIPLE of polarity to move up the ladder of each attribute. To change your vibration and polarity from Lower Attributes into the Higher Attributes, *immediately change the focus of your thoughts.*

The battleground of freedom is any situation where we face a push and pull between freedom and limitation, forgiveness and guilt/resentment, and justice and injustice. Let's look at each type of battleground in turn.

Freedom vs. Limitation

The word "freedom" can be applied in many different ways. Here we are talking about freedom from the illusion of limitation and spiritual bondage that the material world and the physical body can cause us to accept. Because of the level of importance, I will repeat once again that you are a spiritual being living in a material world and not merely a material being striving to have a spiritual experience.

Because the individual soul is housed in the garment of the physical body, the brain (acting as the receptor of the five senses) concludes that our presence in this body is defined by the boundaries of the physical body. Unfortunately, when we define who we think we are by the limited feedback of the five senses alone, we feel separated from everyone and everything around us. But if we change our definition to include our spiritual aspects, our self-perception changes, and then the illusion of separation drops away.

By breaking free from this illusionary darkness which suggests that we are only separate physical beings, our consciousness, which is not limited to the physical boundaries of the body, allows us to reconnect with the Higher Self and therefore, to God. Being disconnected from the Higher Self is only a perception. We never really are disconnected. So when we say *re-connect*, this is only a statement to illustrate getting back to an original state.

> *And he who sent me is with me; and my Father has never left me alone.* (John 8:29)

Give yourself permission to seek God so that you may once again understand your true nature. Will your consciousness to expand beyond the perceived limitation and bondage of your physical body. Take care of your physical body, for it is the garment that you wear for the present moment. But shed the illusion that you are the garment. You are not the body anymore than you are the shirt and pants that your body wears.

How do you expand consciousness and reclaim the spiritual freedom that is your true essence? Through will power. You *will* an expanded spiritual consciousness into your being. Awareness grows from within the soul.

There is a magnetic attraction, which feels like a pulling of the soul towards God. This may manifest in your life as the feeling and thought, "There has to be more to life than this." The realization that the material aspects of life have not brought about lasting joy or happiness is often described as a feeling of something missing.

Some people liken the process of moving towards spiritual freedom and awareness of oneness with God to being woken up from a dream. They begin to see their lives as a series of opportunities to expand their consciousness. They "put on" the mind of Christ after they peel away the veil of illusion that the dualistic, material world has dressed them in.

As we learn to quiet the mind, the Higher Self begins the process of leading us to learn and experience what we need at the right time. Being led to read this book would be an example of this process. Nothing happens by chance.

As we move beyond the limitations of our five senses, our perception of freedom expands in proportion to the expansion of our consciousness.

Forgiveness vs. Guilt/Resentment

> *"Where there is forgiveness, there is God Himself."*
> (Sikhism. Adi Granth, p. 1372)

Earlier, we discussed guilt as one of the main weapons of the Lower Self. Guilt is aimed at the self. Resentment is similar; however it is aimed at other people. Forgiveness is the polar opposite of both guilt and resentment; it's the highest rung on this Attribute Ladder.

Forgiveness of self and others is far easier when we view all people, including ourselves, as spiritual beings living out their experiences for their own reasons.

Guilt and resentment are tools the Lower Self uses to make us prisoners of the past. Forgiveness, which flows from the Higher Self, allows the shackles binding us to the past to be released, allowing us the freedom once again to live in the present moment.

When we were young, most of us were taught that we *should* forgive others. We were taught that forgiveness was the right thing to do. However, only a few of us were actually ever taught *how to forgive*. The art and grace of forgiveness flow out of an awareness that we are all individual souls of one Spirit. Acts that occur as a part of our material life dramas cannot harm the Higher Self we share.

It is my observation that the severity or degree of any issue that's being forgiven affects the ease or difficulty in forgiving. In other words, it appears that it is easier to forgive small offences than severe offences. The need to forgive is largely based on our perception of a situation and how we process or think about a perceived offence.

Here's a frame of reference that may help as you work your way up the Attribute Ladder of forgiveness. I heard this story in passing years ago. I am not sure of the name of the original author, but I remember being profoundly impacted by it. Perhaps this story will give you a new perspective, too.

The Little Angel is a child of God in heaven thinking about the aspects of divinity she'd like to experience in her earthly life to come. She determines that she would like to experience the aspect of divinity known as forgiveness. She goes to her spirit guides to inform them of *her decision*. Being wise, her guides tell her that wanting to experience forgiveness is a very good thing to choose, however, for her to be able to *experience forgiveness* in her upcoming life, she needs to find someone who will hurt her or cause her pain in some way. The Little Angel hadn't really thought about that part of her decision. So she considers who she might find who would be willing to do something in her future life experience that *gives her the opportunity to experience forgiveness.* Just then, one of Little Angel's spirit friends comes up to her and says he will help her experience forgiveness. She is very excited!

Soon after this, another spirit friend, having heard the first conversation, comes over and says that she'll help the Little Angel, too. Just in case the Little Angel forgets, and does not experience forgiveness with the first friend, the second friend will do something in her life to give her a second chance to remember to apply forgiveness. Well, the Little Angel thinks this is great and she's excited to be able to experience the divine aspects of forgiveness firsthand. In her excitement, her two friends stop her and say they'll only help her under one condition: when the friends do something "bad" to her in her next life, the Little Angel *won't forget who they really are* (other little angels and God's children). The Little Angel says she appreciates their help so much that during her life she won't forget who her friends really are and she promises to forgive them.

You can see, this story offers us a loving way, perhaps a new perspective, to view another person who has hurt us in some way. In this case, as odd as it may sound, the Little Angel could also be *grateful* to her friends *for providing the situation* in which she can practice forgiveness. You see, their souls were working together for a common good.

As we have experiences in our lives, perhaps experiences you may be having in *your* life right now, look beyond the obvious outward appearances of things and consider, like the Little Angel promised to do, that more may be going on at a deeper, soulful level.

Here's an excerpt from the book *Radical Forgiveness* (Global 13 Publications, 1997) by Colin C. Tipping, which I have taken great inspiration from as well.

> *There is no need to figure it out. Just be willing to entertain the idea that something else is going on* [at a deeper level] *is a giant step forward. In fact, the willingness to see the situation differently is the key to healing. Ninety percent of*

healing occurs when you become willing to let in the idea that your soul has lovingly created this situation for you. In becoming willing, you let go of control and surrender it to God. If you can really understand at a deep level and surrender to the idea that God will handle this for you if you turn it over to him, you won't need to do anything at all. The situation and your healing will both get handled automatically.

Forgiveness is a paradoxical concept. To forgive someone else of a wrong—whether real or imagined—involves many assumptions. One assumption is the thought that the event around which forgiveness is being given was not meant to occur. At a higher level, another assumption is that the event was *not* brought about, or created, by the person who feels harmed. In my opinion, both assumptions are false.

If an event were not meant to occur, it simply wouldn't have occurred. But if it did, there has to be a root cause or a meaning to the event. It may sound foreign or counterintuitive to you, but consider, as in the Little Angel story, that your soul may have lovingly created this very situation for you to experience no matter how painful it feels or how resentful or guilty you feel. What we do as a result of the experience makes all the difference in the world.

I am reminded about the following passage taken from *The Book of the Prophet Isaiah,* reminding us that God's ways are commonly different than our ways.

> *For my thoughts are not like your thoughts, neither are my ways like your ways, says the Lord. For as the heavens are higher than the earth, so are my ways higher than your ways, and my thoughts than your thoughts.* (Isaiah 55:8–9)

In order to fully understand and apply this lesson, let us clear up some common myths and misconceptions about forgiveness. One of the most common misunderstandings I'd like to correct is that if we forgive another person for something the person has done, within the act of forgiving we are somehow letting the other person "off the hook." In other words, because we forgive someone, that person no longer has to face any spiritual consequences connected with the perceived wrong. Deep down inside (often unspoken), many people believe this is so, and it bothers them so much that they struggle to forgive, or even refuse to try. The trouble with this view of forgiveness is that it stems from a fundamental failure to understand the law of cause and effect.

Surrounding any event that causes us to feel resentment, I would encourage us to separate the two very distinct issues of forgiveness and spiritual law. Let us look closer into these two parts of forgiveness.

The first part has to do with forgiving another of a perceived wrong. Even if the forgiving is in regards to another person, it is a very personal event. Forgiveness helps us and allows us to facilitate the freeing up of thoughts and emotions that have held us in a state of mental and emotional bondage. The very act of harboring and carrying around (in some cases for many years) stored up resentment, hurt, anger, frustration, guilt, or even hatred affects *us* far more than it does the other individual.

The blockages that have been created by stored up thoughts and emotions of resentment begin to fall away. Built-up blocks, narrowing or restricting the down pouring of light, begin to shed with each heartfelt act of forgiveness. We will experience an immediate lightness, like a burden or weight being lifted off of our shoulders.

The second part we need to look at has to do with the law of cause and effect. Where forgiving of others and asking for forgiveness is within our power to choose, administering justice is *not* our role. The law of cause and effect balances consequences, including consequences to others of their actions. As stated earlier, based on our limited, finite perspective, we are not in the position to judge people or hand out consequences. There is a perfect law set in place by God that takes care of things automatically. All we need to do is simply turn the issue over to God.

Forgive us our offences, as we have forgiven our offenders.
(Matthew 6:12)

It may be helpful to view the preceding passage from *The Gospel of Matthew* as a type of equation. In this equation, we could translate the "as we" part into "in equal portion." With this in mind, we would read the passage to mean, "Forgive us our offences in equal portion as we have forgiven our offenders." We are forgiven, in like measure to our forgiveness of others. Forgiving others opens up the door for others to forgive us when we offend or harm them.

Please understand: Forgiveness is *not* saying that what someone did that caused the hurt, the pain, is no longer important. Forgiveness is *not* forgetting or denying a wrong and acting like something never happened. Forgiveness is *not* saying that now you agree.

Forgiveness, my friend, *is* saying: "I know that some of the things that you did in the past *are not a true reflection of who you really are.* I release this circumstance and event and no longer give it any power in my life. I no longer define myself by these events.

At the same time, I release all the thoughts and emotions that have built up and surround this person and event." Forgiveness, my friend, *is* saying: *"Forgive them Father for they know not what they do."* (Luke 23:34)

When we forgive, we are saying: "Father, I trust that you know best. I know that I do not see with the same clarity and perspective that you do. Although I may not completely understand it, I realize that this event is perfect in your divine plan and exactly what my soul needs at this time. I don't know what else to do with it, Father. I am turning this over to you in your infinite wisdom. Here it is. It is now yours."

We must seek only to get to a place of expanded consciousness, a place of a wider perspective, a place that is beyond the ego's investment in the perceived wrong.

Forgiveness opens the door to healing.

Justice vs. Injustice

When calling to mind the battle of justice verses injustice, I am once again reminded of the passage I quoted earlier from *The Book of Isaiah* 55:8–9. In this passage, Isaiah is calling to mind the truth that God's mind creates, operates, and brings events into manifestation from a higher place, from an eternal perspective. Within our human minds, our human reasoning, that which we may view as justice or as injustice is really a result of our limited, finite perspective from which our opinions flow.

At any moment, my perception of what is "just" and what is "unjust" is a function of my current state of consciousness. So much of the suffering, disappointment and discontent I experience in my life stems from the expectations and demands I put on life. Simply put, internal suffering is being in conflict with what is.

It is common to expect certain outcomes in life to occur *our way*, and when they don't, we often experience frustration. Feelings of injustice occur when we experience life in a way that's different than we thought it *should be*. Often when we cannot reconcile an event in our minds, we conclude that the event was not just.

It may be difficult to accept at times, but when we experience "injustice" in our lives, what we're really saying is that we cannot *see* justice being served in a given situation from our finite perspective. That's why we conclude that injustice is being served.

Justice, meaning what is fair, proper, and right, is subjective based on our individual perspective. When we suggest that something is "unjust," we are stating that the something is not *supposed to* happen in this way. This type of thought process runs counter to the spiritual laws, especially the law of cause and effect.

Earlier, when discussing the distinctions between the fear-based thought system and the love-based thought systems, we spoke about judgment and acceptance. Clearly, for us to consider something "just" or "unjust," we had to form a judgment that goes beyond the observation of what is. Remember, we can stop ourselves one step short of judging by just observing. Not judging something as "unjust," does not by default mean that you agree with, or are in favor of supporting it. We can always choose to take action in life, even without first passing judgment.

Perhaps it may be helpful to consider this: Justice, as well as injustice, are superficial judgments. They are generalized judgments. This type of judgment does not consider or get underneath the issue itself. It is much like the analogy of the iceberg. The portion of the iceberg that is obvious and visible is only the small tip of the whole iceberg we can see above the waterline. The majority of the mass of the iceberg is below the waterline, imperceptible from above. So it is in the case of events we label as "unjust." There is always far more happening under the surface than what is observable from above.

Utilizing our mental and emotional energies to judge what we cannot see or fully understand is a choice. We can, however, make a different choice. We can choose to place our trust and confidence in the spiritual laws. God can see the whole story, including the parts of the iceberg that lie outside our view. Spiritual laws handle events in perfect ways, in God's way.

I am he who searches the minds and hearts; and I will give to everyone of you according to your works. (Revelations 2:23)

Those who will rise above and succeed in the battle of justice and injustice will be:

- Slow to judgment.
- Aware that there may be more going on under the surface of events than is obvious and observable.
- Placing their trust in God, who knows how to balance what must be balanced.

Prayers

Use the following prayers to assist you in winning your battle of freedom.

A Prayer for Freedom from Limitation

Father, I thank you for removing the illusion of limitation by granting me awareness and the freedom that comes from knowing that I am a spiritual being, your Divine Child, living and experiencing in a material world. Let it be done in perfect ways and under grace. Amen.

A Prayer for Forgiveness

Divine Father/Mother, through your grace you have opened my mind and my heart to the divine aspects of forgiveness. Through forgiveness of self and others, I am freed from the bondage and blockages that guilt and resentment can create. Forgiveness enters my being in perfect ways and under grace. I trust that all is in divine order. Amen.

A Prayer for Justice

Father, you have granted me the clear perception to see that justice flows from divine law. There is no punishment or reward. There is perfection and balance of energies within your divine spiritual laws. Amen.

CHAPTER 19

Victory #3
Service

"A natural expression of love is service. By helping others we expand our love beyond ourselves, so that it takes on a more universal quality. We begin to love as God loves."
—Timothy Freke

Higher Attributes

Peace/Harmlessness
Brotherhood
Selfless Service

Lower Attributes

War/Violence
Malevolence
Selfishness

APPLY THE PRINCIPLE OF polarity to move up the ladder of each attribute. To change your vibration and polarity from Lower Attributes into the Higher Attributes, *immediately change the focus of your thoughts.*

The battleground of service is any situation where we face a push and pull between peace/harmlessness and war/violence, brotherhood and malevolence, and selfless service and selfishness. Let's take a look at each type of battleground in turn.

Peace/Harmlessness vs. War/Violence

The natural abode of the Higher Self exists in a state of peace and divine harmony within the universal presence of God—the very essence of all that there is.

You'll notice that the nature of the Higher Self, divine harmony, grows within your being the more you overcome the various challenges of the Lower Self by moving up the Attribute Ladders. Looking at life from the perspective of the Higher Self, the more the Higher Attributes source our thoughts, words, and actions, the more we experience inner peace. Peace is the absence of internal conflicts.

In reality, the attributes of the Higher Self *are* your very nature. The goal is to make the Higher Attributes your own: manifesting them in your life experiences in the material world.

> *He alone sees truly who sees the Lord the same in every creature, who sees the Deathless in the hearts of all that die. Seeing the same Lord everywhere, he does not harm himself or others.* (The Bhagavad Gita 13:27–28)

All Lower Attributes are driven by the ego. By looking at the challenges associated with winning the seven battles of the Divine Child, you can clearly see that if a person were functioning every day at the level of the Lower Attributes, a likely effect is that the person's thoughts and behaviors would be defensive and fearful, and express the need to be right by making others wrong. In other words, a person functioning on the lower rungs of the Attribute Ladder would live in an overall state of disharmony.

Over the centuries, when challenges posed by the Lower Self were not overcome individually and collectively, as a group or as a nation, they led to war and the killing of other human beings. Violence fuels additional pain, anger, and hatred. Thus, war, whether it is a conflict between individuals or nations, does not fuel understanding or peace. In our wildest imagination, and despite our most skilled, advanced rationalization (which, sadly, often uses various sacred texts for justification), none of us believes killing another human being is really God's desire. Why would one part of God want to kill another part of God, when both are parts of the same whole? The only reason for warfare is the ego's desire to be right by trying to show others that they are wrong.

We all possess the will power and self-control to express peace, starting in our own lives, with our own *personal wars*. First, we can be a catalyst in cultivating the energy, the vibration of peace, in our own lives. Then, one at a time, leading up to millions of people, we can collectively cause the energy of the world to shift towards peace.

As we turn our attention towards our own personal lives, we may find our own *personal wars* blocking us from experiencing the peace that is our true nature. (This is the same peace that your soul yearns for.) What robs us of inner peace?

- Our self-imposed expectations of others
- Keeping everything inside; not speaking and acting based on our own truth
- Trying to live up to other people's expectations for us; not giving ourselves permission just to be who we are
- Living with the erroneous mindset that "I am not good enough"
- Spending mental and emotional energy in various lower-attribute states, such as guilt, fear, despair, hopelessness, resentment, and scarcity, to name a few

Peace and harmony begin in the inner world, the world of the mind and emotions, and then flow to the outer world. Therefore, let me simply ask: Are there any *personal wars* keeping you from experiencing peace in your thoughts and feelings today? Personal wars are internal conflicts staged on the rungs of a particular Attribute Ladder, they manifest as a pushing and pulling battle between the Lower Self and the Higher Self.

When you succeed in identifying your *personal wars*, if any person or anything aside from yourself comes to mind, you should put on the brakes, and then ask yourself a few questions. Your questions could sound like:

- What is it that this person or event is triggering within me, which is causing me to rob myself of peace?
- Am I carrying a grudge, resentment, or anger inside?
- Have I *made up* some expectations for other people's behavior and choices, and am I measuring them against these imposed expectations?
- Am I trying to live up to other's expectations of me, through which I am not giving myself permission just to be who I am?
- Is there an opportunity to practice forgiveness with this person or situation?

Allow me to add, if you are in a situation that is mentally or physically abusive, or harmful in any other way, pray to the Father. Slow down the mind so that you will perceive God's guidance and then work towards remedying the situation. Potentially, a component of remedying the situation includes removing yourself from the situation.

If one person is being abusive towards another, realize that the abuser is playing a role on the stage of life, one that flows from the Lower Attributes and does not represent a true reflection of who the person really is. Although this may be difficult to accept, pray for the abuser first. Ask God to show the person the way, to open the doors for a solution to manifest into the person's life in perfect ways and under grace.

If you are allowing the absence of peace to persist in your life, on evaluation you'll find that the majority of your attention is being spent living in the past or projecting into the future. Peace, my friend, exists in the present moment.

In summary, as we bring forward the Higher Attributes of our spiritual nature and blend these into our everyday lives, we experience harmony and peace within.

Peace be with you and in you!

Brotherhood vs. Malevolence

For ages, the concept of brotherhood (gender neutral) has been referred to in the sacred scriptures of different wisdom traditions. However, when we observe the state of our current world, it would appear that the concept of brotherhood has not reached everyday application.

Malevolence is a byproduct of the same illusion of separation we've spoken about many times before. When we live our lives unconsciously, reacting only out of past patterns and habits, we buy into the illusion of separation. Not only does this illusion make us believe that we're separate from God, it makes us feel separated from our true spiritual nature. Furthermore, we progress through life believing that we're separated from other human beings. Through an *"us and them"* paradigm of exclusion, the ego promotes the opportunity for us to consider treating other people with ill will, or malevolence. Even the term "ill will" points to a sick or unhealthy use of our energy and free will.

It is not surprising, in virtually all cultures and religious traditions, to find some version of the Golden Rule: Treat others as you would like to be treated. This concept is not a new revelation. In fact, few people would take issue with it. The difficulty with the Golden Rule is not our agreement with, or our understanding of the concept. The difficulty is in the consistent application of the Golden Rule in our everyday lives. So until we change our paradigm towards one of brotherhood, we will constantly struggle to embrace the thoughts, words, and actions that flow out of viewing everyone as us.

The spiritual truth of oneness with God is, in my opinion, under taught. But even when it is taught to us, or we read or hear about it, for most of us it takes time to *really* understand it: time for it to soak in, time to fully embrace it. The concept of oneness goes against the grain of what the Lower Self believes to be true, for it operates as a separate being. Integrating the truth of oneness requires a form of re-scripting our beliefs. But isn't this what all the spiritual masters from so many traditions have invited us to do?

Periodically, I will hear someone say, "My God," in such a way that suggests that his or her God is somehow different than "your God." While it's true that there are many different cultures in the world, and that different members within each culture observe (in most cases) several different religions that have different names for God, this "my God/ your God" talk belongs in an elementary school. Underneath all of creation there is only one God: our God.

As a simple analogy, consider that in various languages, we have a variety of names for the force of gravity, but there is only one gravitational force. We have many names for the Sun, but the Earth is lit, warmed, and nourished by one sun. Similarly we have many names for God, but we all live within one God, sustained by the love of one God, and at the core of our being, we're made in the image of one God. It is through the creative thoughts, the words of this one God, that each of us as individual souls—parts of the whole of God—came into being. Just as we are all children of God, we in turn are all spiritual brothers and sisters.

Believing in the erroneous notion that you are somehow separated from all that there is fuels the erroneous notion that you are separate from other children of the one Father/Mother God. When we are able to move above the ego, we can truly grasp the concept of brotherhood and apply it into our everyday lives by moving away from the paradigm of separation and move towards a paradigm of oneness in God.

In the paradigm of one God, no one is a stranger. No matter how different, we all hail from the same spiritual family. When teaching the paradigm of oneness—that we are all a part of the same whole—Master Jesus taught us the following:

> *For I was hungry, and you gave me food; I was thirsty, and you gave me drink; I was a stranger, and you took me in; I was naked, and you clothed me; I was sick, and you visited me; I was in prison, and you came to me. Then the righteous will say to him, Our Lord, when did we see you hungry, and feed you? Or thirsty and gave you drink? And when did we see you a stranger, and took you in? Or that you were naked and clothed you? And when did we see you sick or in prison, and come to you? The king then will answer, saying to them, Truly I tell you, Inasmuch as you have done it to one of the least of these by brethren, you did it to me.* (Matthew 25:35–40)

As parts of the same whole, what we do to and for others, we do to and for ourselves.

Selfless Service vs. Selfishness

Perhaps greater than in any other area of our lives, when we perform acts of selfless service we can feel the holy breath breathe on our indwelling divinity. Selfless service is providing some form of assistance or support to another person without being asked and without expectation of receiving anything in return.

Being a Higher Attribute, every act of selfless service is born from God. Service is a natural expression of love towards others.

At some point in your life, now or in the past, it's likely that you've performed acts of selfless service, and have in turn, experienced the sensation of radiance, as if an ember has been breathed upon and is glowing within you. This feeling is the vibration of the light of love. At the time, you may or may not have been able to place the source of the warm feelings you experienced. But this higher vibration made you feel empowered, energized, and touched you at the very core of your being.

> *Through selfless service, you will always be fruitful and find the fulfillment of your desires: this is the promise of the Creator.* (The Bhagavad Gita 3:10)

When discussing selfless service, we can relate it to the law of giving and receiving. You will notice that this law is *not* called the law of receiving and giving. Giving comes first. *All of life is a process of giving.* Although perhaps counterintuitive, there is much truth in the saying, "We receive only that which we give away." The more we give away, the more we open the door to receive.

Intentions play a key role in giving. When we're at a higher rung on the Attribute Ladder, we do not give in order to get. We give away kindness, love, friendship, healing, and support, as well as resources like time and money. We give freely, daily, because we understand the concept of abundance and do not operate within a mindset of scarcity.

> *Give, and it will be given to you...For with the measure that you measure, it will be measured to you.* (Luke 6:38)

A great way to go through the day is to ask, "What can I give away today? How can I be of service to others?" Will it be a smile? A kind word? By asking ourselves these questions, we focus our attention on looking for opportunities to give selflessly.

You see, we have to move beyond the "me" of everyday life in order to move towards acts of selfless service. This is not an activity left for some future day when we *have more time.* My friend, this day of *having more time* will never come. The world around you, as well as your Lower Self, will provide you with sufficient reasons to pass, move on, be too busy, or not have in your field of awareness opportunities for acts of selfless service. Proactively seek out opportunities to be of service of others.

Be ever mindful of *selfish* service. Service done with the intention of recognition or of raising a person up in the eyes of others is nothing more than serving the ego.

> *Give simply because it is right to give, without thought of return, at a proper time, in proper circumstance, and to a worthy person, is enlightened giving. Giving with regrets or in the expectation of receiving some favor or getting something in return, is selfish giving.* (The Bhagavad Gita 17:20–21)

As discussed earlier, living life with an abundance mentality (vs. a scarcity mentality) allows us to move towards service to others and away from service only to ourselves.

Furthermore, when we view selfless service through the lens of oneness, we see our service to others as also serving the God within our fellow spiritual brothers and sisters.

> *Let brotherly love remain in you. And forget not hospitality towards strangers; for thereby some were worthy to entertain angels unawares.* (Hebrews 13:1–2)

Lastly, allow me to add yet another powerful way in which we may view service. This comes in the form of establishing your own personal ministry.

What Is a Personal Ministry?

We all are being called upon by God. This call is not audible. It feels more like a pulling sensation deep within our hearts. Often when we hear the term "a calling," our minds go to the type of calling related to the ministry. Although for some, this well may be the case, for most people, the calling relates to the formation of a *personal ministry*.

A personal ministry is anything you do that is of service to, or lifts up another person. It only takes a small shift in perspective to see your actions through the lens of unity. Some of the things you enjoy and are already doing may be viewed as your ministry. Ministry often comes in the form of sharing a talent, such as music or art. For you, perhaps it is gardening or repairing things, or being a coach or teacher. For some, ministry could be providing kind words or a smile to others, lifting their spirits.

Seeing your activities as a ministry may require only a small shift in your perspective of your job. For example, someone in the health care field may consider caring for the sick as a personal ministry. If one embraces it as such, their whole perspective shifts from one of "I have to go to work," to one of taking time to perform a divine purpose, which generally feels much more rewarding.

So what would it look like if we made the small shift in perspective from just our jobs, or what we do, and move forward is such a way that views what and how we do things, as our own personal ministries? Wouldn't they become our own private missions in life? A personal ministry does not have to be announced to others or advertized openly. This is soul work, intimate work between you and God.

When we stop and listen to the calling within our hearts, we will be led to the work of our personal ministries. Chances are good that you either know now what this work is, or, if it's not readily apparent, you can see traces of it already in your life, like little bread crumbs you dropped for yourself as clues to the path. Now is the time to begin to follow those crumbs.

Reflect on the question, "What is my personal ministry?" Begin to move in the direction from which your soul is pulling on your heart, so that you may lift up, in your own unique way, your spiritual brothers and sisters. When you are energized and feel lighter, as you are almost effortlessly working, you'll know you are on the right path. Serving others, through your personal ministry, is one example of God's love manifesting through you!

Prayers

Use the following prayers to assist you in winning your battle of service.

A Prayer for Peace and Harmony

Divine Intelligence is now operating in me and through me, and it is arranging everything in my life to bring peace and divine harmony into my being, in perfect ways and under grace. Within peace and harmony I seek the Kingdom of God. Amen.

A Prayer for Brotherhood

Dear Father/Mother God, I thank you for opening my mind to the divine truth of oneness. I know that all life is in you God, and that you are in all life. May I grow each day in my understanding of this wisdom in perfect ways and under grace. Amen.

A Prayer for Selfless Service

Father/Mother God, thank you for granting me the courage and wisdom to seek out and perform acts of selfless service to my fellow brothers and sisters, your other divine children. May my eyes be opened in perfect ways and under grace to opportunities to serve those in need. Amen.

CHAPTER 20

Victory #4
Love

"Love is the master key that opens the gates of happiness."
—Oliver Wendell Holmes

Higher Attributes

Love/Divine love
Compassion/Mercy
Kindness

Lower Attributes

Fear/Hatred
Indiscriminate judgment
Meanness/Intolerance

APPLY THE PRINCIPLE OF polarity to move up the ladder of each attribute. To change your vibration and polarity from Lower Attributes into the Higher Attributes, *immediately change the focus of your thoughts.*

The battleground of love is where we face a push and pull between love and fear/hatred, compassion/mercy and indiscriminate judgment, and kindness and intolerance. Let's look at each type of battleground in turn.

Love vs. Fear and Hatred

What is fear? What is hatred? From where do they originate? Answer these questions for yourself and you'll see through the illusions which created them. Fear and hatred are born into the minds and hearts of those whose true spiritual essence, which is love, has been buried deep beneath layers of thoughts and experiences processed erroneously.

Fear and hatred are choices, although unconsciously made ones. Does this surprise you? Many people think that fear and hatred are caused by someone or something else, other than themselves. But, effectively they are caused by us, by our reaction to something. Understanding that every effect has as its mate, a cause, we always have the free will to choose how to respond to any situation in our lives. Whether we choose consciously or unconsciously (based on past patterns), a choice is made about our thoughts and emotions.

Fear and hatred neither originate, nor do they exist outside our own minds. Yes, manifestations of fear and hatred can be observed in the external world, but the cause of these manifestations originates in the hearts and minds of men and women just like you and me. As you read this, remember what I said at the beginning of the book: The truth will set you free, but in the process, you may become slightly uncomfortable.

As we're discussing the Lower Attributes of hatred, fear, or at a slightly higher rung on the Attribute Ladder, anger, let me make the observation, when I'm watching the news on TV reports of behaviors that flow out of anger, hatred, and fear, they appear to be pervasive. And when the coverage of such events makes up the majority of what we're exposed to day after day, week after week, what effect do you think this type of communication and exposure has on our individual and collective consciousness? It's like a pounding hammer of negativity. This is a battleground of love.

On any given day, on a percentage basis, how much news and mass media airtime is given to topics and people demonstrating some form of the Higher Attributes? Would you say the percentage is in the single digits? Imagine the shift in energy and perspective, as well as the shift in our individual and collective consciousness that could be created if the media flip-flopped and increased the percentage of time they predominantly reported on events, activities, and people engaged in things that are manifestations of love, kindness, compassion, forgiveness, healing, hope, and selfless service. There are a lot of great organizations—and all of the people behind them—doing things every day that model these Higher Attributes. Those would grow in our consciousness. It would be like light spreading through the darkness.

As an example: We often hear about the kids *in trouble*, and we hear far too little about youth engaged in activities that are clearer reflections of who they really are. What if we were exposed, instead, to countless numbers of events and people demonstrating aspects of the Higher Attributes? The light of these people and events would occupy our thoughts, influence how we feel, and become the topics of our conversations with others. Manifestations of the light of these Higher Attributes would begin to spread like wildfire.

In the meantime, we can choose to be thoughtful of what we feed into our minds and where we hold our conscious awareness. It has been said, "If I change my mind, I can change my choices; if I change my choices, I can change my outcome; that is, I can change my life."

The energy that we create from a mental state of disharmony, such as fear and hatred, will, if held onto for an extended period of time, produce numerous forms of disease in our physical bodies. Fortunately, the mental and emotional distress produced by fear and hatred can be lessened and changed in an instant just by being aware of, and therefore choosing to change our perspective.

You may choose to expand your perspective by applying the steps of self-mastery that we discussed in chapter 14: Calm your mind. View your life's experience through an eternal lens. Apply your knowledge of the spiritual laws. Make the Higher Attributes your mental map. And accept that you are one of God's children. This way, no matter how angry or afraid you feel, you will create an expanded perspective of the situation at hand. Your perspective of any situation can be transformed in such a way that it changes your very thoughts, thus changing your energy and allowing you to consciously choose to move up the Attribute Ladder towards love.

Some folks hang on to their anger as if it were a prized possession. If you're holding onto anger, I would ask, "Who is your anger helping? How does this anger you hold, serve your highest good?" Get underneath the issue and discover the purpose of the anger. By doing so, you hold the very key to freeing yourself from your own self-imposed bondage.

Through the practice of meditation, the calm-minded person is slow to anger. That is another method you can use to climb the rungs of the Attribute Ladder.

Turning our attention now towards the highest end of the love/fear polarity, we find divine love. Divine love is unconditional, meaning there are no conditions for it to exist. Divine love is not subject to our physical limitations, or to our narrow perspective of what is. Divine love does not judge, condemn, or punish. Divine love, in reality, ultimately, is all there really is.

We can catch glimpses of divine love by observing some of the information that is available regarding the life of Jesus and other spiritual masters who consciously embodied the Higher Self. Master Jesus's entire message to us was about love. Simply put, his message to us was to love God, love family, love friends, love strangers, love enemies. And, of course, let us not forget, it was to love ourselves.

In *The Gospel of Matthew* (23:36–40), Jesus was asked:

> *Teacher, which is the greatest commandment in the Law? Jesus said to him, Love the Lord your God with all of your heart and all of your soul and with all of your might and with all of your mind. This is the greatest and first commandment. And the second is like to it, love your neighbor as yourself. On these two commandments hang the law and the prophets.*

As we unfold the paradigm of our oneness with God, we grow to recognize that these two commandments about love are really saying the same thing.

It appears to me that we are hard-wired within our souls to seek God. Some of us have felt this calling deep within us, like a magnetic pull toward God for some time. Others are now beginning to recognize the longing and stirring within to better understand and know our Divine Parents.

Love is both a noun and a verb. We feel God's love and it is also an action. Divine love manifests in our world so that we can recognize it. In our earthly life, the manifestations of God's love can be witnessed in our love for God's other divine children, our spiritual neighbors, if you will. Showing our love for each other is how we can love the Divine within another person (be it friend or foe); it is one way we can manifest God's love into our everyday lives.

> *To love is to know Me, My innermost nature, the truth I am.* (The Bhagavad Gita 18:55)

What better source to turn to for understanding love than the feminine aspect of God, the Divine Mother, for guidance. Here is a message I received from the Divine Mother during a meditation. Listen to what she is telling us about love.

A Message from the Divine Mother

My Love is instilled in the hearts of all men and women. My Divine love can burn away all of the perceived burdens in life as you know it. Love is a natural state of being that many seek outside, but cannot find. When my children open the door, through conscious intention, they will my love into the doorway of the heart. This love is not forced upon any of my children, but when asked, I show them how to regain access to this chamber of love housed within the soul. It is but a doorway which many have forgotten and therefore locked away for some future date.

When this door is opened, the love from within flows outward and influences rightly all matters of living in the world. You need but ask. This secret, which seems so easy to re-gain one's natural state, but so hard for some to realize. Listen to the words and see the deeds of the masters that have shown this truth since the beginning.

My child, you may use these words as a loving, friendly reminder, to all of those who will listen. The locks on the doors, having been created by the self—self-imposed locks you may say—will dissolve away like dust in the wind when you call on the Divine Mother for help in re-gaining this aspect of your true nature. You can gain access to all that is rightly yours from day one.

Fear nothing. I cannot see nor conceive of fear; hatred is but a word I cannot recognize. Neither really exists from my point of view. How could a child of God actually fear or hate anything? Yet it happens on your world, but as easily as it happens, it can un-happen!

As the flow from the Metatron [the Christ, the Higher Self] *comes down—as a stepping down of energy that is consciousness from God—into the awareness of man, more will realize their oneness with God.*

May the glory and love of God shine brightly in the hearts of all of his children. Peace reigns for eternity.

Referring back to the principle of polarity, we can constantly be moving up the Attribute Ladder from fear, hatred, and dislike toward love. Every time we move up a rung, we are gaining a clearer, broader understanding. When we hold ourselves within the understanding that God *is* love, and that we all live, move, and rest our beings in God, we can conclude that the core of us, our true essence, is also love.

When we view love as the *cause*, we see that the Higher Attributes are the *effects*. In other words, love is the cause, forgiveness is an effect. Love is the cause, selfless service is an effect. Love is the cause, healing is an effect. Love is the cause, peace is an effect. And so on. Let those who have ears to hear, hear, and those whose hearts are open for understanding, understand this principle.

As we shift our thoughts, words, and actions to be more aligned with the Higher Attributes, the vibratory energy of love will spread and grow in our lives. The darkness of fear and hatred cannot exist in the presence of the light of love. What would the world look like if each of us individually practiced transmuting this one attribute of fear or hatred into the Higher Attribute of love? Allow me to answer this question for you. It would look like what we picture "heaven" to look like. We would create heaven on Earth. As the Bible reads: *"Thy will be done on Earth as it is in heaven."*

You can experience this victory in your own world right now, because it begins moment by moment with each decision you make!

As shared in the message from the Divine Mother, we need but ask through clear intentions for Divine love to be awakened within us.

> *Ask, and it shall be given to you; seek, and you shall find; knock and it shall be opened to you. For whoever asks, receives; and he who seeks, finds; and to him who knocks, the door is opened. Who is the man among you, who when his son asks him for bread, will hand him a stone? Or if he should ask him for fish, will he hand him a snake? If therefore you who err, know how to give good gifts to your*

sons, how much more will your Father in heaven give good things to those who ask him? (Matthew 7:7–11)

Our everyday lives consist of challenges. Some of these are big; some small. We regularly come face to face with such challenges as financial concerns, emotional troubles, sickness, relationship conflicts, and the like. Sometimes, when we need it most, at times when we feel most challenged, for a variety of reasons it is difficult to ask for help. We feel as if there's an unspoken rule that we must struggle through our challenges alone. Fortunately for us, God is never too busy to hear from us. We can always pray. We can always ask for divine intercession.

Continue to seek, continue to knock, and continue to ask. Break through all of your self-imposed barriers until you feel the presence of God enfold you with her love. Then you'll be closer to claiming your divine inheritance.

Compassion/Mercy vs. Indiscriminant Judgment

The hardened heart demonstrates little to no empathy for its fellow brothers and sisters. Indiscriminant judgment is born out of the darkness of ignorance, which believes through self-delusion that not only are we separate from God, but that we are separate from one another as well. Often we judge other people based on our perception of their outward appearance or behavior, as filtered through our ego-created standards. In fact, there appears to be a constant urge to judge and label people and events going on around us. Where does this urge to judge and label come from?

When we judge and label based on our own limited perception of reality, quite unknowingly we create a degree of disharmony within ourselves. In relation to the other person we're judging and labeling, we can ask, "What is this soul's history? What is this soul's journey? What aspect of God is this soul trying to experience?" If we are unable to answer these questions in full, we come face to face with the realization that judging others is a pointless exercise, unless of course, it leads us up the Attribute Ladder toward compassion and mercy.

> *Judge not, that you may not be judged. For with the same judgment that you judge, you will be judged, and with the same measure with which you measure, it will be measured to you.* (Matthew 7:1–2)

When we indiscriminately judge other people and situations *without* the commensurate presence of compassion and mercy, we can be assured that we are functioning from the perspective of the Lower Self. In actuality, our judgments are nothing more than our personal opinions, though they may be stated as facts. It is unnatural, if not impossible, for compassion and mercy to flow out of a mind filled with anger, hatred, or fear.

We have the ability to become conscious observers, stopping one step short of declaring judgments. Being a conscious observer and stopping short of passing judgments does not mean, by default, that you agree with certain behaviors or situations. It means we separate the perceived issues and behaviors from the true Self that lies within those we would judge. We become conscious observers every time we utilize our awareness to observe what is, rather than simply reacting to people and events in our lives.

It is difficult to practice compassion and mercy when we are focusing only on ourselves. We must step aside, and rise above the "I, me, and mine" self-references of our minds in order to allow compassion and mercy to rise within us.

On the opposite end of polarity from indiscriminate judgment is the pole of compassion and mercy. Compassion is deep awareness of the suffering of another, coupled with the desire to relieve the suffering. Mercy is a disposition to be kind and forgiving of another. *Both* compassion and mercy flow out of love. When we operate our lives within the love-based thought system, we observe and experience kindness, compassion, and mercy flowing naturally from ourselves to others. This is true of all of the Higher Attributes; and we all have them within us.

Through our experiences, some of these Higher Attributes rise to the surface, while others may be hidden beneath layers of built-up pain or suffering. Even if some of the Higher Attributes are hidden for the moment, rest assured that they are still inside of us because they are the natural essence of who we are. We need only to remember the Higher Attributes, to be woken up to them, and to bring them back to the surface.

When we allow our hearts to do our thinking and feeling, compassion and mercy begin to happen quite naturally, as is demonstrated in our everyday lives in the form of our compassionate and merciful thoughts, words, and actions. As we touch into, and are guided by the Higher Self, these Higher Attributes come through us and manifest in our lives.

> *When a person responds to the joys and sorrows of others as if they were his own, he has attained the highest state of spiritual union.* (The Bhagavad Gita 6:32)

Kindness vs. Meanness/Intolerance

Being kind to others is one of the many things our elders taught us as children. However, we did not all learn the lesson well, for when we pause and become objective observers, it does not take long to observe, hear, or read about various unkindness and intolerances in our lives or in the world at large.

I start from the perspective, that at the core, all people are kind— even those who demonstrate unkindness, as most of us have at one time or another. We like and appreciate it when others are kind to us. So when and how does meanness and intolerance set in? As we grow up and our beliefs are formed, if we are not mindful we can, little by little, become intolerant in varying degrees of people we perceive to be different from ourselves.

It appears that when the pace of life is moving fast, when we are running from here to there and juggling our seemingly endless list of things to do, our minds are running at the same speed, jumping from topic to topic. The nature of the racing mind is reactivity. The reactive mind, when confronted with challenges and obstacles (perceived or real), more times than not resorts to a defensive posture. From this defensive and reactive mindset we say and do things that we would not normally say or do to others otherwise.

Reflect on it. Have you ever said or done something and then, later, when you were in a calmer state of mind could not believe what you said or how you acted? I am guessing that most people have had this experience.

The *secret* to much of what we're talking about in regard to the seven victories can be achieved by cultivating a calm, even mind. A calm-minded person will develop his or her self-awareness and self-mastery faster than a person who has a racing, anxious, reactive mind.

When you look around, you will see that much of the world's unkindness and intolerance stems either from a reaction to another or from the need to be right (thus from making someone else wrong). This mind is characteristic of the Lower Self. Unkindness and intolerance flow out of, and are effects of functioning within the fear-based thought system.

As we gain mastery over our thoughts and emotions, we have a far greater likelihood of expressing kindness through our thoughts, words, and actions. Kindness is not a strategy or technique. Being kind comes from within, from operating in alignment with the Higher Self. Kindness, therefore, is a state of *being*, before it manifests into acts of *doing*. With every act of kindness, unseen layers hiding the Higher Self from us fall away. Kindness, much like unkindness, is a choice; therefore we must choose kindness each day in thought, word, and action.

Prayers

Use the following prayers to assist you in winning your battle of love.

A Prayer for Love

Father/Mother God, your divine love flows to me and through me, as my true nature is a reflection of your love. Your love surrounds and enfolds me, eliminating all traces of fear and hatred in my life. God, it is in perfect ways and through your loving grace that this transformation takes place within me now. Amen.

A Prayer for Compassion/Mercy

My Divine Parents, through your grace, you have shown me that the attributes of compassion and mercy are a part of my true nature. May your love, which brings forth compassion and mercy, flow through me toward my brothers and sisters in perfect ways and under grace. Amen.

A Prayer for Kindness

Dear Father/Mother God, through your grace you help me to live each day within the love-based thought system of abundance, acceptance, and being in the present moment. Your kindness, which flows through me, manifests in my thoughts, in my words, and in my actions in perfect ways and under grace. Amen.

CHAPTER 21

Victory #5
Power and God's Will

*"I had such a hopeless desire for you till I saw
how your light yearned for me too. I pushed and
I pushed till I saw it was you who had already
drawn me to every good that I knew."*

—Rumi

Higher Attributes	Lower Attributes
Power/God's will	Human will
Faith	Doubt
Courage	Helplessness
Humility	Pride/Arrogance

Apply the principle of polarity to move up the ladder of each attribute. To change your vibration and polarity from Lower Attributes into the Higher Attributes, *immediately change the focus of your thoughts.*

The battleground of power and God's will is any situation where we face a push and pull between power/God's will and human will, faith and doubt, courage and helplessness, and humility and pride/arrogance. Let's look at each type of battleground in turn.

Power/God's Will vs. Human Will

Through faith, you can allow the power and God's will to influence your thoughts, words, and actions. This requires having the courage not to rely solely on our own human will, but to surrender and have faith.

> *Trust in the Lord with all your heart, and do not rely on your own insight. In all your ways acknowledge him and he will make straight your paths.* (Proverbs 3:5–6)

Here enters the dichotomy of individual free will and God's will. It appears that we have been given the gift of free will. We have the ability to believe, think, feel, and act independently. At the same time, we are expressions of God and never really separate.

Upon learning the concept of free will, we next come to a place in life where we're exposed to the concept of surrendering our will to the will of God. We have the realization that although we have free will and may respond to life as we choose, we have no real control of anything in life except for our own thoughts. The bottom line is that we only have the freedom to choose the direction that our *will* influences our minds in order to focus our attention (therefore, our energy) in a particular manner.

The phrase *"Thy will be done on Earth as it is in heaven,"* speaks to the topic of putting aside our free will in order to move in divine harmony with God's will here and now. To surrender our will, which is largely driven by the Lower Self, to the will of the Higher Self is no easy task. The Lower Self is accustomed to being in the driver's seat. It does not take kindly, at least initially, to the suggestion of someone else being in the driver's seat.

The secret of surrendering comes in the form of marrying, or blending, the Lower Self and the Higher Self, into one. We'll discuss this in more detail in chapter 24, "Union of the Two Selves." For now, let me just propose that, we actually receive independent will in order to someday abandon it in favor of living our life under the influence of God's will.

A question that may be going through your mind right now is, "How do I recognize God's will?" First, let me say that the ability to differentiate God's will from the will of the personality is directly related to your ability to quiet the racing thoughts of your conscious mind. When you learn to quiet your mind, you'll be better able to differentiate the voice of God's will from other thoughts.

You will be able to recognize God's will because you know that it corresponds to the Higher Attributes you've been reading about at the beginning of each of the chapters on the seven victories of the Divine Child. Being able to still those racing thoughts is a critical first step, however. Practicing meditation will help you to quiet your mind.

The world will try to influence you to doubt that you can turn things over to God and flow in harmony with the current of God's will. Doubt comes from a variety of sources. Sometimes this influence comes from individuals who are well intended, but haven't yet crossed the threshold of higher consciousness, self-awareness, and faith themselves.

Our beliefs, although largely formed early in life, continue to form and crystallize over time based on our experiences and information we gather. The set of beliefs that we hold at any moment in time make up our *mental map*. Remember, our mental map acts as a type of filter by which we pass through, and process new information and new experiences.

Human reasoning, our capacity to form intellectual and emotional conclusions, in large part is a byproduct of the limited perspective that the physical senses give us, also combined with our personal experiences. In other words, reasoning is a function of the brain based on a narrow bandwidth of information. It is the process by which we pass information and experiences through the filter of our mental map and develop opinions and conclusions. These opinions and conclusions are often taken as facts, or reality, when in fact they are really only a result of the makeup of our current mental map.

For example, two people with distinct mental maps can experience the same event in their lives and then develop opinions and form conclusions that are very different. Their perceptions of events (how they think and feel) can be drastically different.

When our mental map has been formed with components of the fear-based thought system, the ego strives to protect and preserve what it believes to be true. This is the ego's perception of "reality." If our mental map is comprised of Lower Attributes, then it is common that we will filter information and experiences through these attributes and manifest them in the form of decisions, opinions, and reactions that are consistent with the nature and makeup of our lower-attribute mental map.

It's a gift to understand that we can change the nature of our mental map filters whenever we make a conscious decision to do so; it means we can improve them.

The process of *transforming* the nature of the mental maps through which we define ourselves and our life experiences can, in some cases, happen instantly. In other cases, transformation may take some time; we need to convince the subconscious mind through repetition to replace an old part of the map with a new part. In a sense, we can liken this process to *re-programming* our subconscious mind to accept new ways of viewing things.

I will not pretend for moment, nor will I try to portray, that I completely know or understand God's will. Certainly, I wouldn't know God's will for your life. Instead, I am simply offering a way to look at the topic.

> *One God and Father of all, who is above all and through all and in all of us.* (Ephesians 4:6)

God is the All in all. God is, all that there is. Nothing exists apart from or outside of God. Everything that exists, whether unmanifested or manifested, exists inside the presence of God. Therefore, if God is all that there is, what more could God possibly want? I suggest that *God wants nothing.* To suggest in our minds that God wants something implies the notion that God must be lacking something. But how could everything lack something?

Although we may not entirely understand God's will, we can catch glimpses of it, as it has been described by spiritual masters throughout the ages. We can perceive, believe, and use certain attributes as a guide of God's will.

- To love God is to love our brothers and sisters (our spiritual neighbors) as ourselves
- To forgive others is how God forgives us
- To live in loving service to others

God's divine will is to know him and to be like him. God's will is for life to express itself. Through the expression of life itself, be it in the physical or spiritual worlds, we can see the face of God. The expression of God's divine will manifests in one way, through consciousness of the Higher Self.

Allow the flow of the universal energy of God's will through the Higher Self to assist you in victory during all aspects of the seven battles of the Divine Child. Simply let go and let God lead the way to the best of your ability.

Faith vs. Doubt

We have all had times in our lives when we have experienced both faith and doubt. Doubt largely stems from three things.

- Feeling (and belief) in separation from God
- Not understanding the spiritual laws
- Over reliance on the five physical senses

Feeling (and Belief) in Separation from God

The feeling of separation stems from the notion that you are separate from God. That God is "out there somewhere" and not right here, right now. This is an illusion, as we've seen. This illusion is so tightly woven into the assumptions that we make that we often no longer question it. Historically, people have thought about God similarly to the way they see themselves and other human beings, with our eyes. Our physical eyes tell us that we are separate from each other. I am here, you are over there. Therefore, over time, we have expanded this *separation thinking* to include the Divine.

Developing and increasing faith comes much more easily to us when we hold the belief and perception that the presence of God is right here right now, and not only abiding in some far-off location that we call "heaven."

Faith leads to trust. Trust leads to knowing.

Not Understanding the Spiritual Laws

Not having an understanding of spiritual laws can lead us to doubt. We come to question various occurrences in life—things we cannot reconcile—if we do not have a foundational understanding of the following spiritual laws, as they are defined in *The Kybalion* or by this author.

- The law of love
- The law of cause and effect (aka the law of karma)
- The law of vibration
- The law of continuous life (aka life eternal)
- The law of attraction
- The law of giving and receiving (aka the law of compensation)

When we acquire a greater understanding of these Hermetic principles and spiritual laws, we find it far easier to move towards a state of deeper faith, deeper trust, and an awareness of the whole versus awareness of the parts exclusively.

Over-reliance on the Five Physical Senses

Relying too heavily on our physical senses causes us to *buy into the illusion* that God is somewhere else, because we do not see God with our physical eyes, hear his voice with our physical ears, or feel his touch on our physical skin.

> *The foolish do not look beyond physical appearances to see my* [God's] *true nature as the Lord of all Creation.* (The Bhagavad Gita 9:11)

In regard to the physical senses, let us take just one, our sense of sight, as an example. Many people believe only in what they can see. Based on information that I've learned, the human eye sees less than 1 percent of the *known* electromagnetic spectrum. Can you see the microwaves as they cook your food in your microwave oven? No. But do you doubt the existence of microwaves because you cannot see them? No. Can you see radio waves as they travel through the air to and from your cellular telephone or another wireless device? No. Do you doubt that they exist? No. We do not doubt the existence of microwaves or radio waves because we can witness their outcomes.

Because we can only *see* less than 1 percent of the *known* electromagnetic spectrum, does this mean that the other 99 percent does not exist? Of course not. Relying only on our five senses traps us in the illusion of separation. They keep us trapped in the material world, occupied by ego-self created material and emotional issues of the day.

We are spiritual beings living in a material world. We are immortal souls encased in the shell of mortal, physical bodies. Therefore, as we move beyond reliance on our physical senses, we open the door to the spiritual world where our faith can be transformed into knowing. Truly, it is when we move ourselves beyond the reliance of our physical senses, into the application of our non-physical senses, that the doorway to life beyond the physical world comes into our awareness.

> *Truly I say to you, Unless you change and become like little children, you shall not enter into the Kingdom of heaven.* (Matthew 18:3)

In the absence of doubt, only faith and knowing remain. So remove doubt and have the faith of a child.

Courage vs. Helplessness

Courage is the quality of mind or spirit that allows a person to face difficulty. Courage comes from within. You may need courage to seek and consider new truths and new beliefs, and question some of your old ones. Pray to God that you will have the strength to harness the courage to pursue victory over the Lower Attributes.

Helplessness only occurs so that you may experience and understand it. This is not to say you must remain in that state. Helplessness and the emotions that come from this mental state are caused by a belief in separation, a belief that you are *out here all alone*. You may *feel* alone from the viewpoint of being by yourself or from feeling trapped in various life circumstances, but this is not to say that you need to feel helpless at the same time—unless, of course, you *choose* to feel helpless. A feeling of helplessness can only exist in our imaginations.

The feeling of being helpless is an effect of some other cause. Continue to question and unravel the mystery of what that cause may be. You must harness the courage within to question yourself. Oftentimes, writing questions on paper focuses the mind, rather than to race from topic to topic. Through this process, you will learn that you yourself are the creator of this state of mind and feeling, which is based on your own perceptions. You need not judge yourself harshly for creating this state, only to learn from it. You have been asking yourself questions all along whether you were conscious of it or not. Change the focus and nature of the questions you ask yourself and you'll notice that your perspective changes, too. In many cases, changing the nature of your self-imposed questions from "why" questions to "how" questions, is all that's needed to produce a shift in perception.

In an effort to change our inner state of being, self-imposed questions should focus on the present, not dwell on the past or fears about the future. Feelings of helplessness and hopelessness can only remain alive when we are living in memory and/or projecting made-up scenarios into the future.

When you've had quite enough of helplessness and hopelessness, reach into your store house of courage and, through the will of the Divine within you, allow new thoughts to arise. These new thoughts create new energy, which, in turn, acts as an agent or catalyst for new and different types of actions to manifest into your life. Pray that you've learned enough from this experience so that you may leave this temporary state behind, and move back into the flow of divine harmony. Asking for God's intercession is a key to empowerment.

Consider this: You are a child of God. How could you really ever remain helpless?

Humility vs. Pride/Arrogance

Pride and arrogance, both aspects of the Lower Self, block the connection we have with God's will by clouding our awareness. Pride and arrogance surface in a person when the ego, acting out the illusion of separation from our Father/Mother God, begins to cause the person to think and feel that he or she has developed or accomplished something solely of his or her own accord.

We continue to participate in the game of self-delusion when we *think* that it was we who originated an idea or that it was we who accomplished something all on our own. We mistakenly believe that we, individually, are the doer of deeds.

> *Deluded by his identification with the ego, a person thinks,*
> *"I am the doer."* (The Bhagavad Gita 3:27)

Pride and arrogance are means for the ego to further solidify its sense of having a separate existence. If you ever feel either of these mental states beginning to surface, pause right then and there. During your moment of pausing, ask yourself, "Could I create one fingerprint? Could I create one star in the sky? Where does consciousness arise from?" These questions can be humbling to answer. Once you have reminded yourself that God is the source of fingerprints, stars, and consciousness, you can substitute gratitude for any pride and arrogance you felt before you asked yourself these questions.

If you were to make a short list of things a person may take pride in or become arrogant about, you'll likely notice that the things on the list are temporary, of the material world (not of the spiritual world), and that all are illusions.

Think about the vastness of creation on Earth. Now extend your thoughts to include the known universe and the yet to be discovered universes. Extend further beyond to include everything yet unmanifested. We become humbled by recognizing ourselves as individualized souls within God and all creation. Acting out of our humility, we have the ability to practice gratitude. As Corinne Heline reminds us: "Humility and forgetfulness of self are passwords to the highest attainment."

When we read about spiritual masters from different traditions, they appear to us as being very humble people. Through humility, they demonstrated their belief that the Divine was working in and through them to their followers/students, and that they were not just thinking, speaking, and acting of their own accord. I believe that they were consciously aware of the Divine flowing through them and, thus, they were clearer reflections of the Divine manifesting in human form. A master has the humility to understand and know that his or her role is to serve others, not to be served.

Owe/Own

Many years ago I was taught several mental models that helped me a great deal in my life. One such model was called "Owe/Own." For a while I didn't fully understand it, and even disagreed with it. Now that I fully understand it I can see that it contains wisdom. Essentially, the owe side of the Owe/Own model means that when something *I label* as "positive" occurs in my life, I owe credit for this to someone else. For example, I owe gratitude to our Father/Mother God and credit through spiritual laws for this event or situation taking place. I could not and did not accomplish it solely on my own accord.

The own side of the Owe/Own model means that whenever something *I label* as "negative" occurs in my life, I own this occurrence. It was through my own thoughts, words, or actions that this not-so-pleasant event or situation occurred in the first place.

Simply put, I owe the good in my life (that which is working) to a higher force, and I own the not-so-good (that which is not working). My observation is that many people have these thought processes reversed. They operate (perhaps largely unaware) from the position that when good things occur they deserve credit for them and when not-so-good things occur they blame them on someone or something else.

> *The rulers thought that it was by their own power and will that they were doing what they did, but the holy spirit in secret was accomplishing everything through them as it wished. Truth, which existed since the beginning, is sown everywhere. And many see it being sown, but few are they who see it being reaped.* (The Gospel of Philip)

It is healing to be humble. For example, as a spiritual healer, I am humbled every time God's universal healing energy flows through me as its instrument and performs wonderful healing for others who are in need. I didn't create the healing energy. In actuality, I don't even know exactly how it works. I just *know* it does work and that the energy flows from the one Source and power that heals all.

Seek the higher path of humility and inherit this attribute of the Higher Self.

Prayers

Use the following prayers to assist you in winning your battle of power and God's will.

A Prayer for God's Will and Intercession

Father, I ask for your divine intercession in my life at this time. I thank you for your grace in allowing my mind to become still so that I may be aware of and perceive your divine will. Allow my will and your will, Father, to be one and the same in perfect ways and under grace. Amen.

A Prayer for Faith

My Divine Father/Mother God, I thank you for helping me to increase my faith in you and your divine plan. On a daily basis, open my consciousness to your divine plan so that even during troubled or confusing times, my faith in you acknowledges that all is in your divine order. Amen.

A Prayer for Courage and Strength

Divine Intelligence is now operating in me and through me, and is infusing me with the courage and strength I need to seek and realize the Higher Attributes, which are one with my true nature. May courage and strength be revitalized in my being at this time in perfect ways and under grace. Amen.

A Prayer for Humility

Divine Mother, as I move closer to the realization of the Kingdom of God and my divine inheritance, I am grateful. Thank you for gracing me with your gift of humility as I acknowledge my movement back to oneness with you and all that is holy. Holy Spirit, move within me and grant me a humble heart in perfect ways and under grace. For it is through humility that I come to realize that I am an ever-clearer reflection of your divine will. Amen.

CHAPTER 22

Victory #6
Life Eternal

*Life is eternal. Death is but a doorway
leading into and out of the spirit world.*

Higher Attributes

Healing
Truth/Continuity of life
Abundance

Lower Attributes

Disease
Death
Scarcity/Poverty

APPLY THE PRINCIPLE OF polarity to move up the ladder of each attribute. To change your vibration and polarity from Lower Attributes into the Higher Attributes, *immediately change the focus of your thoughts.*

The battleground of life eternal is any situation where we face a push and pull between healing and disease, truth/continuity of life and death, and abundance and scarcity/poverty. Let's look at each type of battleground in turn.

Healing vs. Disease

While we could make a list of the various reasons that people get sick, from inherited and environmental conditions, to karmic reasons (whether caused by choices in this or a prior lifetime) and soul reasons, such as assisting in the life lessons of another person, it would appear that the *cause* of the majority of illness and disease is our mental state and habitual thought patterns.

By and large, illness is not caused by our *conscious choices*. After all, who really wants to be sick? Certainly, I mean no disrespect to anyone who is sick or has suffered from any form of illness or disease. However, the habitual mental and emotional patterns and corresponding vibrations that appear to cause most illness and disease in our physical bodies are fear, anger, hatred, criticism, resentment, and guilt. The energy of such thoughts and emotions creates disharmony in our subtle energy bodies, which, in turn, manifests disharmony in the cells of our physical body resulting in illness and disease.

Earlier we discussed the power of our thoughts to create and attract. The greater the separation in *time* a cause is from its corresponding effect (in this case illness and disease being the effect), the less likely we are to make the connection between the cause and its corresponding effect. Oftentimes, destructive thought patterns have been with us for so long that we are unaware of them. When we do not recognize these disharmonious thought patterns, we are no longer able to recognize their presence in our lives.

For health to be restored, in addition to relying on professional medical attention for treatment, it is wise to seek healing at its root level. We may have experienced situations or experiences that caused us pain that we buried in the form of fear, anger, hurt, resentment, and guilt under our conscious everyday thoughts instead of dealing with it. It is through dealing with these emotions and changing how we process these experiences mentally that allows us to properly eliminate them from our subconscious mind. Suffice it to say, to reverse disease we need to shift from the fear-based thought system to the love-based thought system.

There are times when a person has fallen ill and he or she has been cured with the help of the medical community. However, with much disappointment, the person finds that he or she has another illness within a relatively short period of time. Because the person worked to eliminate the illness but did not work on eliminating its root cause, the same or a different physical condition resulted. That is, because the person did not change his or her mental map, habitual thought processes, and emotional state, illness was repeatedly manifested.

Of course, if we abuse our bodies from poor diet or lifestyle choices we can cause health issues. Beneath these behaviors, there are mental and emotional states that correspond to the fear-based thought system. When we work on healing the underlying cause, moving up the Attribute Ladder by way of the spiritual laws and prayers for divine intercession, the effects in our bodies must be healed as well.

None of this is saying that if you are sick, you should not seek professional medical help. You should. At the same time, you can work on healing the cause as well. My heartfelt wish is to pour out and direct healing energy from the one Source and power that heals all, to you, and all those in need if you and they are not well.

As stated earlier in describing the steps of self-mastery, we need to harness our self-awareness and our intuition as our tools when we're in the process of uncovering the underlying causes of manifested illnesses.

Truth/Continuity of Life vs. Death

One of the greatest fears that people have is the fear of death. It is my observation that this fear stems from:

- The unknown (or apparent unknown).
- Teachings about sin, final judgment, and hell.

In *The Bhagavad Gita* (2:11–12), Sri Krishna admonished us that we have nothing to fear regarding the so-called mystery of death. He assured us that there was not, nor will there ever be, a time when our existence ceases. Clearly he spoke in terms of the spirit and not the physical body.

> *The wise grieve neither for the living nor for the dead. There has never been a time when you and I and the kings gathered here have not existed, nor will there be a time when we will cease to exist.*

This expanded, immortal perspective—which is mirrored in all major religions—allows us the opportunity to remove any notion of fear and doubt that we could somehow fail to realize our divine nature in our journey through life. We cannot fail to realize the nature of the Higher Self and our oneness with God. It is not a question of *if* we can succeed, only *when* we will succeed. *When* we succeed in realizing our unity and oneness with God is a matter of individual choice.

Krishna goes on to describe the eternal, immortal state. What is impermanent, contrary to the limits of what our five senses tell us, is not reality.

> *The impermanent has no reality; reality lies in the eternal.* (Bhagavad Gita 2:16).

> *The body is mortal, but he who dwells in the body is immortal and immeasurable. … As a man abandons worn-out clothes and acquires new ones, so when the body is worn out a new one is acquired by the Self, who lives within.* (Bhagavad Gita 2:18—22)

Just as birth into our physical life is but a doorway we step through from our spiritual abode and into the world, death, as we call it, is but a doorway we step back through when we leave our physical bodies. It is unfortunate that this change is called "death." The word itself denotes an extinction of life. The truth is that spiritual life continues on after the transition called death; albeit in a different form, consciousness lives on.

In the second chapter of *The Bhagavad Gita,* Krishna also provides a glimpse of what we must experience in order to pass from mortal death to immortality, as opposed to passing from mortal death to rebirth.

> *They are forever free who renounce all selfish desires and break away from the ego-cage of "I," "me," and "mine" to be united with the Lord. This is the supreme state. Attain this, and pass from death to immortality.* (The Bhagavad Gita 2:71–72)

Sri Krishna was pointing out that we can be free from the cycle of birth and death when we "break away" or abandon the ego personality and become united with the Higher Self.

Throughout *The Seven Victories of the Divine Child* we have been expanding on the teaching of *breaking free* from the impermanent appearance of a separate existence and provide a process for moving forward into unity and oneness with God.

The Unknown (or Apparent Unknown) of Death

Many people are waking up to the misguided teachings that you only have one shot at this thing we call "life." People are waking up to the oddness of the notion that an all-merciful and loving Father/Mother God would provide us with only one chance to obtain a level of spiritual maturity sufficient to reawaken to our oneness with God. For the most part, this belief of *one lifetime* is founded largely in the West or Westernized religions elsewhere.

In *The Gospel of Matthew* (5:48), Master Jesus taught:

Therefore become perfect, just as your Father in Heaven is perfect.

The grace of our Father/Mother God *allows* for rebirth of the soul into new bodies (often referred to as reincarnation). And it is through the rebirthing process, which brings the soul from the world of spirit into the physical world for another go-around, that we can correct our past errors when in our past lives we *missed the mark* or sinned, if you will.

It may be helpful to reframe or define what we mean when we say "death." In one sense, you could say that we die to the world of spirit when we are reborn (or reincarnate) into the physical world. And we die to the physical world as we are reborn into the world of spirit. These worlds differ only in the degree of their subtle vibration.

However, I prefer to think about death in this way. We are spiritual beings having a human experience in a material world. We are not merely material or physical beings trying to have an occasional spiritual experience. Because our true essence is made in the image and likeness of God, which is Spirit, we are spiritual beings. The spirit does not die when it is clothed with flesh, born into the material world. Nor does the spirit die when our physical lifetime ends and the spirit once again separates from the physical body. So you see, from this perspective of spiritual beingness, there is no death, only a change in form. Life continues on. The spirit—who you really are—is eternal.

Transitioning from the physical realm of existence back into the spiritual realm of existence is really nothing more than a change. It is not an end. Death can thus appropriately be thought of as *a doorway of transition between various states of existence and levels of consciousness.*

And Peter asked the master who awakened them, Who are these men who stand beside the Lord? The master said, These men are Moses and Elijah, who are come that you may know that heaven and earth are one; that masters there and masters here are one. The veil that separates the worlds is but an ether veil. For those who purify their hearts by faith the veil is rolled aside, and they can see and know that death is an illusive thing. (The Aquarian Gospel of Jesus the Christ 129:17–19)

Sin, Judgment, and Hell

In further discussing the fear of death, let us turn our attention to the notions of "hell" and "purgatory." Humanity is opening our eyes and beginning to see that the teachings of sin and hell have been misunderstood and/or manipulated over time. I do not judge if these changes were made intentionally or out of a lack of clear understanding. For centuries, beliefs about hell, purgatory, judgment, and fear of God have been taught (and in some misguided cases they're still being taught and accepted today); therefore, they are rarely questioned.

Purgatory is the process *purging* all of the negative energy that was acquired during an incarnation. Fire is used as a symbol of this sacred process. Sacred fire burns off the negative energy and renews the soul. Humanity is now waking up to the teaching that an all-loving, unconditionally loving Father/Mother God placing one of his/her children in hell to burn for eternity is both inconsistent and contradictory.

Can you imagine an earthly mother, with all of her love and compassion for her children, sentencing a child to burn and be tortured in hell for all eternity because of the child's error? All because the child went down the wrong path. If we have a difficult time imagining that an earthly mother could or would do such a thing, than how can we accept that our Divine Parents, who possess eternal love, compassion, and mercy would do such a thing? What would be the point of it? What would it actually accomplish? These types of teachings of sin and damnation to hell have created an environment of a fear of God instead of a love of God.

Now, we would be wise not to confuse the idea of "punishment" with the natural consequences of the spiritual law of cause and effect. The universe is perfect and is always in the process of balancing energy. So please understand, my friend, that when events occur in life that we would label as "*bad*," they are not punishment from God. Instead, these events are the *effect* of our own thoughts, words, and actions, whether these originated yesterday, three years ago, or in a prior incarnation.

> *For truly I say to you, Until heaven and earth pass away, not even a yoth or a dash shall pass away from the law until all of it is fulfilled.* (Matthew 5:18)

Similarly:

> *Truly I say to you that you would never come out thence until you had paid the last cent.* (Matthew 5:26)

Your soul, held within the oneness of God, continues on after the change that we call death. This fact was one of the greatest gifts given to humanity by Master Jesus, who showed, through the resurrection (the restoring of life), that life continues after the change of shedding the physical body.

Referring back to one of the steps towards self-mastery, viewing your life experiences through an eternal lens that's broader than one physical birth and death, can help to lessen and eventually eliminate your fear of death.

Once we move beyond our own fear of death, it is expected that the ego immediately turns our attention, concerns, and fears toward the loss of our loved ones, and thoughts of being away from them when either they or we die. But we need not fear for them. Our loved ones, as sons and daughters of God, continue to remain alive in the presence and care of our Divine Parents. Granted, for a short time, on the timeline of eternity, we may remain in the physical world while their departed souls reside in the spiritual world. However, we are only a thought away from our departed loved ones, separated from them only by a thin, etheric veil.

When we truly believe that life continues on, albeit in a different form, after the change we call "death," we begin to see through the illusion that our existence ends at the point when we dispose of our bodily garment. We can come to the full realization that our true essence, consciousness, and awareness, which are housed within the physical body during our lives, live on.

> *Those who remember me* [God] *at the time of death will come to me. Do not doubt this. Whatever occupies the mind at the time of death determines the destination of the dying; always they will tend toward that state of being.*
> (The Bhagavad Gita 8:5–6)

Our perspective of death is based entirely on which side of the fence we are standing on, the physical side or the spirit side. On either side, death is only the transition from one side to the other. Life continues on after the change called death. Life is eternal. Death is only a doorway leading into and out of the spirit world.

Abundance vs. Scarcity/Poverty

In the context of this book, when we speak of abundance or more specifically of having a mindset of abundance, we are referring to the thought paradigm: "There is enough of everything to go around for everyone." Compare this paradigm with its opposite polarity, a paradigm of lack or scarcity: "There is not enough of something for everyone." The scarcity mentality causes us to focus our attention on lack and doing what we can to get our *fair share*.

Now it is clear to me that we currently live in a world where many people live in a state of lack. Many people lack what we consider to be basic human needs: food, clothing, and shelter.

Beginning with the one thing (arguably, the only thing) that we have individual influence and control over—our own thoughts—we can better help these people. I recognize that there are many organizations whose honorable efforts are dedicated to assisting those areas of our world where people lack the basic human needs. Arguably more can be done to assist those in need. However, for this particular writing, I am talking directly to you, the one whose hands are holding these words.

Three spiritual laws come to mind in working through the larger understanding that is required for the victory of abundance over scarcity: the law of attraction, the law of cause and effect, and the law of giving and receiving. The first, the law of attraction is a vibratory law. It states that like vibrations will attract like vibrations. So if our thoughts (and beliefs) dwell at the "scarcity" or "lack" end of the Attribute Ladder, we will attract more situations, conditions, and events into our lives that support the state of mind of "lack." We are able to break free from this state of lack when we become aware of, and then change our beliefs about abundance and scarcity. We accomplish this when our dominating thoughts move up the Attribute Ladder and focus on abundance instead of what we are lacking.

Through the law of attraction, we begin to attract different situations, different conditions, and different events into our life that are consistent with our new, dominant thoughts of abundance.

The only way to change an effect is to change the cause. In other words, the only way to change the effect (in this example, the state of lack) is to change the cause (thoughts and beliefs about lack) into thoughts and beliefs about abundance. That is the law of cause and effect.

The law of giving and receiving also pertains to abundance. When a person dwells in a state of lack (perceived or real), he or she is less likely to give of him or herself to others, be it the giving of time, money, or resources. In fact, giving when in lack would seem counter intuitive, wouldn't it? Why would a person who is lacking give away something he or she perceives he himself or she herself does not have enough of already? Well, God's laws often run counter to the way we think as human beings in the physical world.

> *For my thought are not like your thoughts, neither are my ways like your ways, says the Lord, For as the heavens are higher than the earth, so are my ways higher than your ways, and my thoughts than your thoughts.* (Isaiah 55:8–9)

Applying the law of giving and receiving requires another ingredient: faith. All of life is a game of giving. There is much truth in the statement, "We receive only that which we give away." We can give away kindness, love, joy, friendship, compassion, healing words, and resources, including time and money. The more we give away, the more we open the door to receiving. Moving into an *abundance mentality* tells us that we do not have less because we gave these things away, but indeed, the opposite is true, we have more.

When we operate our lives from an abundance mindset, we can have faith that through the infinite supply of the universe, all of our needs will be fulfilled. In the very act of surrendering and allowing God's will to influence rightly all matters of living, we open the doors to God's abundance to enter into our lives. In oneness, we all live, move, and have our being inside of the presence of God. With the oneness frame of mind, the giver is also the receiver.

Here is the key: Because energy follows thought, keep your attention and focus on abundance, not on what you perceive to be lacking in your life.

Prayers

Use the following prayers to help you win the battle of life eternal.

A Prayer for Healing

My Father, through you, the one Source and power that heals all, every trace of fear, anger, hatred, resentment, criticism, and guilt is removed from my being. Your light and your love fill every cell and atom of my being. Through your light, Father, the darkness of imperfection fades away. I am made whole through your healing light, which comes to me now in perfect ways and under grace. Amen.

A Prayer for Truth/Continuity of Life

Dear Father/Mother God, thank you for opening my eyes to the wisdom of the continuity of life eternal. I am a spiritual being experiencing the material world. I have no fear of an earthly death, as death does not come to my true essence, which is spirit. My soul is immortal and continues to live on after I shed this physical garment. Amen.

A Prayer for Abundance

I am aware and acknowledge that universal supply is available to me from my Divine Parents. Through my thoughts, words, and actions I give. And through the same I receive, according to my highest and best good. My outer-world abundance is a clear reflection of my inner world in perfect ways and under grace. Amen.

CHAPTER 23

Victory #7
Wisdom and Thought

*"What the superior man seeks is in himself,
what the lesser man seeks is in others."*
—The Analects of Confucius 15:20

Higher Attributes	Lower Attributes
Understanding	Narrow-mindedness
Wisdom	Human Reasoning
Illumination/Enlightenment	Ignorance

APPLY THE PRINCIPLE OF polarity to move up the ladder of each attribute. To change your vibration and polarity from Lower Attributes into the Higher Attributes, *immediately change the focus of your thoughts.*

The battleground of wisdom and thought is any situation where we face a push and pull between understanding and narrow-mindedness, wisdom and human reasoning, and illumination/enlightenment and ignorance. Let's look at each type of battleground in turn.

Understanding vs. Narrow-mindedness

It is my observation of myself and others that there is a natural tendency towards the comfort of consistency in our routines. Most people are creatures of habit. From simple routines, like where each family member sits at the dinner table, to the routine we follow when we wake up in the morning and get ready to start each day, we ritualize many of the repetitive tasks we perform each day. Sometimes we get stuck in a rut by doing the same things over and over each day, no longer giving them any thought.

Our thought processes can get into a similar rut, as if we were simply running on autopilot. With the busyness of the business of life, with the multitude of roles each of us plays every day, it is quite easy to lead an unexamined life. It would therefore appear that leading an unexamined life is a path of least resistance, a comfortable way to travel through life. Switching off the autopilot and leading an examined life, at least initially, can involve some of the hardest work we will ever do.

It is not at all uncommon for a person to be brought up in a family where there is a specific set of beliefs (spoken or unspoken) about religion and spirituality, about God, about life, about death—even a set of beliefs about having no beliefs. No matter what these beliefs are, whether they are articulated and taught or just implied, by and large people will fall into one of two groups. One group will learn the beliefs they are exposed to as children, follow along, and rarely ever question the beliefs, even if some parts don't feel right. As a result, consciously or unconsciously, they will accept these beliefs as their own. They'll move forward in their own lives with these beliefs, and, as adults, rarely examine them in any depth.

The second group of people (some could grow up in the same household) will learn the beliefs they are exposed to as children, begin to follow them, accept the parts they resonant with, and question other parts that simply don't feel right or make no sense to them. As adults, they'll move forward in their own lives with some of the original beliefs and filter in new ones they have acquired along the way.

It's commonplace for people to read and learn something about the sacred scriptures of their particular religious upbringing. It is equally as common for only a small percentage of people to reach out, seek out, and expose themselves to sacred scriptures of other religions. Too seldom do people investigate, and therefore consider, the beliefs of other religious and spiritual belief systems. It is a function of the ego to maintain the position, "If you believe in something that is vastly different than what I believe, then, of course, you, not I, are wrong." The ego deals largely in absolutes; things are either black or white.

On several occasions I've had the privilege to attend classes on the topic of "The Unity of Religion." In these classes we were shown the sacred scriptures of the world's major religions and taught their core beliefs. It does not require being a scholar to quickly see the beauty in each tradition. I remember being struck by the amount of similarities between them, as opposed to differences. Oftentimes, people have a tendency to disagree with what they do not understand. But over the years I have found common threads of truth in all of the sacred scriptures and world religions I've studied.

When we desire to expand our wisdom and understanding, and approach learning with an open mind, we are willing to explore thoughts and information that are, at the time, different than those we have been exposed to.

Narrow mindedness, the unwillingness even to consider other ways of seeing life, life's purpose, and our relationship with God, keeps us trapped inside a small box of beliefs. When we allow ourselves to remain trapped inside a small box of beliefs, we are limiting our growth. Each of us has our own built-in compass if we pay attention to the Divine within us. The guidance we receive from the Higher Self will lead us to what it is that we really wish to learn and experience in this lifetime. Understanding begins with an open mind and an open heart.

The Lower Self's tendency is to remain narrow minded in ways that support and reinforce its current set of beliefs. The Lower Self is not fond of being wrong. The gift comes in the conscious awareness, led by the Higher Self, that the Lower Self does not have to be wrong, but that the Lower Self may just consider another way of looking at something or change a currently held belief. The Lower Self wants to be *either/or,* but it can be shown that there is also another choice: *and.*

Changing the way we perceive life, life's events, or our spirituality does not necessarily mean the old way was wrong. The process of journeying into greater understanding and wisdom does not make everything else we used to feel or believe wrong. That is a judgment. The progress of understanding and wisdom is like walking up a set of stairs towards a doorway; it is progressive. The doorway to understanding opens when we can suspend judgment of the old while we consider new ways and new beliefs.

> *Jesus said, let him who seeks continue seeking until he finds. When he finds, he will become troubled. When he becomes troubled, he will be astonished, and he will rule over the all.* (The Gospel of Thomas, saying 2)

Wisdom vs. Human Reasoning

Although listed here under the heading of the seventh victory, we come across or, let's say, bump up against the battle of self-realization, wisdom, and understanding throughout our journey within all seven battles and all seven victories on the path of the Divine Child. For in reality, these attributes are not as compartmentalized as I've illustrated them here for the sake of communicating about them.

Wisdom is timeless, as it is influenced by the Higher Self. Wisdom raises us up above the "I, me and mine" perspective of the Lower Self, and moves us beyond the finite timeline of this one (our current) life experience. Wisdom, as spiritual insight, assists us by allowing us to peek into the eternal, beyond the mortal playground of the temporal world.

We can access inner wisdom only when the mind is at rest. The anxious, racing, reactive mind overshadows inner wisdom. Internal noise and mental chatter distracts us from hearing the wisdom and guidance coming from within. When inner wisdom seeps through, as it does in an intuitive flash, the mind, when led by the ego, will attempt to justify all the reasons why the wisdom is incorrect. The reasoning efforts sent forth from the Lower Self are attempts to maintain control by utilizing previously accepted information and past experiences as ammunition for its reasoning. This ammunition, in turn, is used as justification for why the wisdom, which is often counter intuitive, was received in error.

> *If any of you lacks wisdom, let him ask God who gives to all men generously, and without reproaching, and it will be given him.* (James 1:5)

It is likely when you think of someone who is "wise," that you'll also notice the same person carries and radiates a sense of peace and calmness about them. When I was growing up, I loved to watch the television show *Kung Fu*. In this show, the martial arts student (played by David Carradine) had a teacher he called "Master." His master was a blind man who exuded wisdom in every interaction. Not only did the master console his student through wise discourses, and often by challenging the student to see a situation from a different perspective, he himself was the best demonstration of a calm and peaceful person that I've ever seen.

Our journey into the realization of wisdom is just that, a journey and not a final destination. As our wisdom and understanding of the mysteries of life and of Spirit percolate into our awareness, new levels of conscious awareness, new levels of wisdom, act as our springboard towards yet higher consciousness, higher knowledge, and higher wisdom.

This journey is about raising the Lower Self up to be in at-onement with the Higher Self, and to reach the point where the two become as one. It is a process of blending our spiritual being with our human being until they are in accord.

As we turn our daily attention towards our oneness with God, which moves us toward the wisdom of the Higher Self, the divinity of our true nature, we point ourselves in the direction of *willing* wisdom into our beings. We *will* the Higher Self, in union with the soul, to open our hearts and our minds to the wisdom that we need in our lives at this time.

We receive wisdom, be it from the external source of a teacher, through written words, or through our inner connection with God. We can feel wisdom and its truth in our hearts. Engraved in the divinity of the Higher Self, which lies within every single human being regardless of race, religion, gender, or social and economic status, is a compass of truth. When we are calm and connected, our souls, in union with the Higher Self, become a type of compass leading us to truth and wisdom, guiding our discernment.

Wisdom and understanding grow and emanate through an expanded awareness and an expanded consciousness, not through a restricted or narrow view of life.

There is virtual assurance that through our *active will* and *conscious striving* we can align our everyday thoughts, words, and actions with the Higher Attributes discussed within these chapters on the seven victories. A person will gain self-mastery, an expanded view of life, and awareness of the Higher Self (Christ consciousness), which is by nature and creation all-wise and all-knowing.

Applying wisdom and understanding to the development of Higher Attributes can *cause* an expanded level of awareness, allowing us to see beyond and through old ways of thinking, feeling, and living. At the same time, the application of Higher Attributes in our lives can have, as its natural *effect,* an expanded level of wisdom and understanding. You see, through the individualized soul, wisdom and understanding of the Higher Attributes can be viewed both as *causes* and *effects*.

Remember, wisdom often runs counter to human reasoning. Wisdom is God's consciousness stepping down into the awareness of men and women and manifesting as the understanding of the unity of God and man.

> *In dark night live those for whom the world without alone is real; in night darker still, for whom the world within alone is real. The first leads to a life of action, the second to a life of meditation. But those who combine action with meditation cross the sea of death through action and enter into immortality through the practice of meditation. So have we heard from the wise.* (Isha Upanishad 9–11)

Allow the wisdom of the Higher Self to guide you, the Divine Child, to victory. And in doing so, you will come to claim your divine inheritance.

Illumination/Enlightenment vs. Ignorance

This author is not particularly fond of the word "ignorance," as it feels harsh. So let us examine the definition of the word. *Random House Unabridged Dictionary* defines it as a "lack of knowledge." That sounds much better.

> *There is no greater wealth than wisdom; no greater poverty than ignorance.* (Nahjul Balagha, Saying 52)

As we journey up the Attribute Ladder from a lack of knowledge to illumination, we become more attuned with the concept of oneness with God. Our entire journey through the seven battles encompasses the process of clearing out the darkness of ignorance. A part of this process is to shine light upon and clarify old belief systems that simply are not working for us any longer. In large part, this is a process of letting go.

The *perception* or *illusion* that we are separate from all that there is, separate from God, peels away. As it does, our eyes are opened, our hearts made receptive, and our consciousness is expanded into knowing that all is in God and God is in all. Nothing exists apart of or outside of God. This is the beginning of understanding oneness.

When the light of our awareness of oneness shines through the darkness of separation, the illusion of separation can no longer exist. As our understanding of oneness grows stronger and brighter, there is a reduction of the importance of self and a growing desire to manifest selflessness (among other qualities) in our lives.

When we study the lives of spiritual masters and sages, we observe the countless selfless acts they do for their fellow human beings. Through their example, the masters and sages of old and of our current day show us a path, a way of *being,* that we can emulate.

Initially, illumination and enlightenment can seem distant, indefinable, and available to only an elite few. I am here to say that the enlightened state of being is available to all of God's children. Yes, this includes you!

Enlightenment can be a paradoxical concept in that you do not directly seek it. An enlightened state of being, defined as complete awareness of oneness with God, is a natural effect of, and flows out of the peeling away layer after layer of ignorance about separation. Although enlightened awareness can happen all at once, through God's grace, it usually happens in phases, as if we are peeling an onion one layer at a time.

Our journey towards a state of illuminated truth is not a race in which some trophy is awarded at the end. It is not a competition to see who among us will get there first. This type of thinking is clearly ego driven. In fact, we have nowhere to go. When we can see through the delusive nature of an apparently dualistic world, we come to realize that we were never separated from the Source, never separated from God in the first place.

> *Know him to be enshrined in your heart always. Truly there is nothing more in life to know. Meditate and realize this world is filled with the presence of God.* (Shvetashvatara Upanishad 1:12)

Enlightenment is likened to coming around full circle to the place where we began only to realize that we are now, and always have been, a part of the same whole and where we needed to be.

I know that there is a part of us that just wants to scream out, "Will someone please just tell me how to get there, just tell me what to do and how to do it!" Words cannot and do not, substitute for the *personal experience* of the light shining in our awareness, illuminating our understanding of our oneness with God. Words can only point in the direction of the thing, not get you there. To know consciousness, seek the one who causes consciousness, and you will discover who you really are.

> *And you will know the truth, and that very truth will make you free.* (John 8:32)

Prayers

Use the following prayers to assist you in winning your battle of wisdom and thought.

A Prayer for Understanding

Divine Mother, thank you for lifting the fogbank of illusion from my perception, and for showing me the doorway to understanding, in perfect ways and under grace. As I go through the doorway of understanding, awareness of oneness with you floods my being. I now realize we have been one all along. I am at peace in your loving embrace. Amen.

A Prayer for Wisdom

O Divine Mother! May I have the wisdom in this hour not to rely on my own limited reasoning. May your wisdom surface in my thoughts in perfect ways and under grace, and serve as a guiding beacon of light in my life. Amen.

A Prayer for Enlightenment

Mother/Father God, my Divine Parents, I am grateful that you have awoken me from the sleeping state of belief in separation, in perfect ways and under grace. I realize now that there never was a moment when we were apart. My entire being is alive in your light and I am one with you in your all-encompassing presence. Amen.

PART SIX

Claiming Your Divine Inheritance

"What the father possesses belongs to the son, and the son himself, so long as he is small, is not entrusted with what is his. But when he becomes a man his father gives him all that he possesses."

—The Gospel of Philip

"But the son is not only a son but lays claim to the inheritance of the father."

—The Gospel of Philip

CHAPTER 24

The Union of the Two Selves

> "When you make the two one, and when you
> make the inside like the outside and outside like
> the inside, and the above like the below, and when
> you make the male and the female one and the
> same ... then will you enter the kingdom."
> —The Gospel of Thomas, saying 22

IT APPEARS THAT A MAJORITY of religions hold within their scriptures and beliefs some epic battle or story of light versus darkness. The victorious process of transformation from darkness into light is evident when we are infused with higher consciousness. As the door of higher consciousness swings open, our eyes are opened to the truth of who we really are. As written in the popular hymn by Clara H. Scott, "*Open mine eyes that I may see, visions of truth thou has for me.*"

If you are still thinking you are the material body that your consciousness and immortal soul inhabit, then your understanding of who you really are is not there yet. If you still think that you are separate from God, then your understanding of oneness is not there yet.

There are two primary guards at the door of realizing who you really are and realizing your oneness with God: Their names are Fear and Ignorance. These two guards are not real; they exist temporarily in the duality of this world. They have no life of their own except for the awareness and energy you give to them.

Earlier we discussed the principle of polarity and the seven victories. When we choose to focus our attention, and therefore our energy, on the opposites of these two guards, their presence blocking the doorway to higher consciousness begins to dissolve. The divine light within us begins to shine on our awareness.

> *The door giving access to this omnipotent and transforming alchemy of the Spirit in man is open to all, at all times, and the key to its opening is in the thoughts of all.* (Life and Teaching of the Masters of the Far East, volume 2)

The process of oneness, of becoming conscious of and at-one with the Higher Self, thus one with God, is less a process of acquiring something new and more a process of letting go: letting go of false assumptions, letting go of our separation paradigm, letting go of the Lower Attributes that keep us stuck in ego identification.

I believe that at the core of all of the "searching" on our *spiritual quest*, be it through religion, spirituality, philosophy, or metaphysics, we are really seeking to reunite with our true and original state of being: oneness with God. All of this searching is like skirting around the outside edge of our real goal, catching only glimpses of it. It's also like having a small taste of a delicious meal, but returning to a place of not being completely satisfied or totally fulfilled in our search. This feeling of not being completely satisfied or totally fulfilled is your soul talking to you, urging you to move forward towards your real goal.

Deep inside, we long for the love we experience when we are alive and at-one with God. We long to experience once again the state of oneness with God we call "home." The longing within the soul that feels like homesickness, causes us to search out and recreate the experience of oneness with God while we are here on Earth.

As a Divine Child, your true state is oneness with God. This is something you've had all along, not something you have to acquire. Claiming your divine inheritance requires letting go of the thoughts and beliefs that serve as a barrier between where you stand now and where you will stand once you realize your true spiritual nature.

United with God

Sri Krishna's teachings provide additional insight on uniting with God. In *The Bhagavad Gita* (4:9–10), we read:

> *He who knows me as his own divine Self breaks through the belief that he is the body and is not reborn. ... Such a one, Arjuna, is united with me. Delivered from selfish attachment, fear, anger, filled with me, surrendering themselves to me, purified in the fire of my being, many have reached the state of unity in me.*

Essentially, Krishna is teaching that we can move beyond the limitations of separation thinking in our lifetime. Our awareness of the Divine within enables us to experience a shift in our perception of God. It helps us to see that God is closer to us than we may have ever realized!

Mystical union with God is possible on Earth, as it is in heaven, as the Bible says. Many people (and perhaps you are one of them) find it difficult to find the words that accurately capture the magnetic pull or attraction they feel in their inner being toward knowing and realizing God. This feeling is often described as *something missing* inside: a hole or a void. In reality, there is nothing missing other than our awareness, or remembrance, of God's presence, which has been with us all along.

> *Fill your mind with me; love me; serve me; worship me*
> *always. Seek me in your hearts, you will at last be united*
> *with me.* (The Bhagavad Gita 9:34)

If we were to view the preceding passage only from a separate, ego-self perspective, it *could* feel like the scripture is saying to love God, serve God, and worship God as a separate being. We perceive an expanded perspective of the previous passage when we accept that we are one with God and that a part of God (the Higher Self) dwells in everyone. Then, we experience our existence, along with everyone else's, inside of God.

"*Fill your mind with me.*" We can allow our thoughts to be occupied with the omnipotent, omnipresence of God in the following ways: love, service, worship, and seeking. When we acknowledge the Higher Self within us, then we acknowledge it within everyone else, too. It would be foolish to pretend, even for a moment, that God's divine presence is housed only in certain people and not in others.

Through the viewpoint of the Higher Self, who shines light on our awareness that reveals our oneness with God, the phrase "Love me, serve me, worship me, and seek me" takes on a whole new meaning.

"*Love me*" means to love one another: meaning, all people. This leads us to see beyond the outward appearance of others, and love the Divine within them, which is who they really are. Since God is in all people and we all live inside of the presence of God, then loving each other is a manifestation of God's love in our lives. This does not mean we have to agree with others' behaviors. We must suspend judgment. Remember, God causes the sun to shine upon the good and bad, and rains on the just and unjust alike.

"*Serve me*" means to serve each other. Selfless service to others is a manifestation of serving God. When we serve others, we serve the God within them.

"*Worship me*" means to honor the God within each person. We possess the ability to see beyond the obvious outward appearances of others and honor the Divine within them. Many times, however, due to our limited perspective we label and judge people's behavior when we do not know their souls' history or purpose. This judgment is not worship. We shouldn't just worship God during the time we are attending a church service. We should worship God all day long in how we treat our fellow spiritual brothers and sisters. From the perspective of the Higher Self, we can love, serve, and worship what we know to be at the core of every person: the Higher Self or Divine presence within them.

"*Seek me*" means to continue to take steps toward God by realizing God's presence in our everyday lives. We can seek God by arriving at the house of quietness in mind, knock on the door of that place with pure intentions, and keep on knocking; God hears us and opens the door in due time.

When we choose to apply these and other wisdom teachings into our everyday lives, we put ourselves on a path of conscious unity with God.

> *God has declared: I am close to the thought that My servant has of Me, and I am with him whenever he recollects Me. If he remembers Me in himself, I remember him in Myself, and if he remembers Me in a gathering I remember him better than those in the gathering do, and if he approaches Me by as much as one hand's length, I approach him by a cubit. If he takes a step towards Me, I run towards him.* (Hadith)

Blending of the Two Selves

Each of us is on a unique path towards the realization of our oneness with God, the path of claiming our divine inheritance here and now. All paths lead to one God. All paths invite us to bring our spiritual nature to the forefront as we live our daily lives, in this moment, and in our material world. This, indeed, is what the spiritual masters have modeled for us to observe. You, my friend, are a Divine Child, a master in the making.

Although many people compartmentalize their lives into times when they perform their spirituality and times when they perform everything else required for maintaining their existence, I invite you, as many have done before, to blend these two parts of your life together into one whole.

> *Awake, O sleeper and rise from the dead, and Christ* [the Universal Divine Child/Higher Self] *shall give you Light.* (Ephesians 5:14)

The union of the two Selves—the Lower Self and the Higher Self—begins when we move from the stage of learning into the stage of integrating the teachings covered in the prior five parts of this book. In all likelihood, you have already started the process of integration.

Our expansion in consciousness, or resurrection in thought, does not happen only by reading books and scriptures or by attending a weekly religious service. I'm not suggesting that we stop doing these things; just that we move beyond these steps into daily integration of these spiritual teachings.

> *I hear and I forget. I see and I remember. I do and I understand.* (The Analects of Confucius)

Union of the two Selves is a way of living in the world. Initially, it is a conscious process of *willing* the Higher Attributes of our spiritual nature into our human experience, so that life for us will be on Earth as it is in heaven. When we call upon and acknowledge the Higher Self, the Christ, the Atman within us, we begin the process of reunion of the two Selves. We move ourselves up the Attribute Ladder toward embodiment of the Higher Attributes each day. Our movement is evidenced by our very own thoughts, words, and actions every day.

In the scriptures we read about this movement, this transformation in consciousness from lower to higher, from what was our "old" self into a "new" self. In *Paul's Letter to the Ephesians,* Paul wrote that the objective of spiritual growth is to put away the "old man," meaning our old ways of thinking, speaking, and acting in the world, and bring forth the "new man." We read:

> *Lay aside all your former practices, that is to say, the old man. ... And be renewed in the spirit of your mind, and put on the new man* [the Universal Divine Child/Higher Self], *who is created by God in righteousness and true holiness.* (Ephesians 4:22–24)

Paul also alluded to our transformation in consciousness when he wrote:

> *Do not imitate the ways of this world, but be transformed by the renewing of your minds.* (Romans 12:2)

Although the process of living in the material world and experiencing victories in the areas we discussed often feels like a battle, we can make peace between the Lower Self and Higher Self. A natural outcome of blending the two Selves into one—and thus, bringing forth the "new man"—is the experience of flowing in divine harmony and knowing firsthand the inner peace that passes all understanding.

As we blend our spiritual being with our human being, and bring them into one accord, someone will need to be in the driver's seat of our lives. Someone will need to be the leader. In all likelihood, this will require changing who is in the driver's seat today. We can consciously change the driver of our life from the Lower Self, and invite the Higher Self, the Christ, the Atman within, into the driver's seat.

> *And call no one on earth, father, for one is your Father in heaven. Nor be called leaders, for one is your leader, the Christ* [the Higher Self]. (Matthew 23:9–10)

Our minds are renewed during the transformation process of ushering the "new man" into the driver's seat of our lives. During the process of renewing your mind you'll notice a change in the nature and makeup of the filter of perception known as your mental map. The new man's mental map consists of the Higher Attributes, nearer to consciousness of our natural state of unity with God.

It is truly a sacred marriage when we blend our spiritual being with our human being into one accord. In doing so, we prepare to receive our divine inheritance!

CHAPTER 25

The Divine Manifests in Life Through You

*"When I was a child, I spoke as a child, I understood
as a child, I thought as a child; but when I
became a man, I put away childish things."*
—1 Corinthians 13:11

To echo Paul's statement from 1 Corinthians above, when I was a young boy I thought as a child. Similar to the way God is depicted in the movies, I pictured God sitting high up in heaven. And when he spoke, I imagined it would sound like a loud, booming voice, perhaps accompanied by some thunder and lightning. His appearance, when he showed up, would be majestic to say the least.

As my thinking matured, I came to realize God was the opposite of what I had thought and pictured as a child. This childish view of God was transformed. I came to realize that the presence of God is not only *out there someplace*; instead, the presence of God is in and around us, and manifests as life and consciousness. I came to learn that God does not talk in a loud, booming voice; instead, God speaks to us all of the time in a quiet, still, small voice. I learned that the question wasn't *if* God was talking to me, but if I was listening to God (or even expecting to hear God). Since God spoke in a still, small voice, I knew I'd have to learn to quiet my mind enough so that I could perceive this divine voice.

How are you expecting God to show up in your life? Whether or not you are expecting God to show up, plays a large role in where you look for him. At this stage in our development, we do not see God in his *unmanifested* form. However, we can see and experience God all around us through his manifestations. When we are attuned to the Divine manifesting through nature, through other people, and through ourselves, our perception is heightened, allowing us to experience things that we might otherwise have been blind to. When our perception is attuned in this manner, we travel through the day as observers, with both eyes open.

Here is an example of the Divine manifesting in plain sight. I was driving my car recently and had just pulled up to a stop light when I noticed an elderly man in a motorized wheelchair at one of the four corners of the intersection. Then I watched as another driver across the way from me got out of his car and started walking through the traffic towards the elderly man. As this gentleman approached the elderly man, I saw him bend over to pick something up from the street near the curb: the elderly man's hat. Apparently, the hat had blown off of the elderly man's head as he was crossing the street. He'd been trying to get back to where his hat lay on the ground when this other driver put his car in "Park," got out, and walked through the traffic to pick up the elderly man's hat and hand it back to him. After handing him his hat, the driver simply waved to the elderly man and ran back to his car just in time for the light to change. Observing this very quick episode of kindness, I felt like I had just been given the gift of observing God manifesting his love. In my car, I thanked the kindly gentleman in my heart, and I thanked God for allowing me to have both eyes open.

You won't see this gentleman's act of kindness on the evening news. Nor will you read about it on the Internet. Nonetheless, this and countless similar scenarios unfold before our eyes every day. They occur in every town and city. Sometimes we're aware of them. Other times we're too busy doing our own stuff to notice them.

As we become ever-clearer reflections of the Divine within and have a firm understanding of who we are at essence, our thoughts, words, and actions become, like the kindness of the gentleman in my anecdote, a manifestation of God in the world.

Every day from now on, I invite you to ask yourself a question that I term the "Priceless Question," which is: *How will the Divine manifest through my life today?*

There is power in the Priceless Question. It breaks down the perceived walls of separation. It directs our attention as we begin the day, attuning us to the presence of the Divine within us and to the presence of God manifesting in the life we see all around us. Setting an intention to allow the Divine to manifest through our thoughts, words, and actions creates space for us to make choices that express the reality of our oneness with God.

Embracing unified awareness and renewing our mental maps in accordance with the Higher Attributes causes us to move forward on our journey of being an ever-clearer reflection of the Divine. When we combine our spiritual being with our human being, the Divine manifests through us so we may experience it and others may see it.

Your soul longs to experience God while it is still housed in the physical body. Your soul longs to feel, to experience the presence of God—his Kingdom—on Earth as it is in heaven. The doorway is open for you to perceive the Kingdom of God right here and right now. Personally experiencing oneness with God is life altering. Like looking through the eyes of a master, by knowing and communing with the Higher Self, you will perceive yourself, the physical world, and the spiritual world, in ways you've never dreamed of. Everything that exists will be illuminated.

May your soul find rest and peace in oneness with God. This, my friend, is your divine inheritance. Claim it now.

Conclusion

*"This awakening you have known comes not
through logic and scholarship, but from close
association with a realized teacher."*
—Katha Upanishad 1.2:9

WE HAVE COVERED A LOT of ground in this book. Arguably, any single section of it could fill a volume of its own if written about in detail. Perhaps, if Spirit leads me in that direction, various sections or topics in this work will be expanded upon in later books. I allow the Divine to be in the driver's seat, leading me to what needs to be communicated.

As I shared in the Introduction, I am here only as a messenger. The vast majority of the material presented to you in this book has been "spiritually inspired." That is, it has flowed from Spirit, through me, in order that Spirit may share this message with you.

Still your mind in me, still your intellect in me, and without doubt you will be united with me forever. If you cannot still your mind in me, learn to do so through the regular practice of meditation. If you lack the will for such self-discipline, engage yourself in my work, for selfless service can lead you at last to complete fulfillment. If you are unable to do even this, surrender yourself to me, disciplining yourself and renouncing the results of all your actions. (The Bhagavad Gita 12:8–11)

For most, the spiritual path to higher consciousness is a process. Aside from divine grace granted by our Mother/Father God, I am not aware of any "quick fixes" to use as pathways to higher consciousness. True knowledge, which is based upon direct personal experience, is required in order to allow higher forms of perception to enter your awareness. The spiritually mature person learns how to tune-in and discern higher consciousness, which is available to all of us.

I trust that you have experienced changes in perception and in your understanding of who you are, as you've been reading this book and exploring the principles it covers, in addition to becoming aware of your close connection with the Divine.

It is time for us to move *beyond* merely "believing" in God. It is time for us to move ourselves into a place of "knowing" God. *The Seven Victories of the Divine Child* is a modern-day revelation, allowing us to move into this place of "knowing." By unraveling key divine mysteries and pulling together the silver threads of truth found in various world religions and mystery schools, we can finally progress from a state of believing to a state of knowing and experiencing oneness with God here and now.

Always remember, you are a spiritual being having a human experience. Our spirituality, our spiritual nature, is not just one aspect of our life; it is the umbrella encompassing all aspects of our life. Within this paradigm, everything we think, say, and do flows out of our true spiritual nature.

The spiritual guidance contained in this work is timeless. As I've stated previously, I am confident that as you apply these teachings the benefits that you experience in your life will be profound and real.

When you take the personal responsibility necessary to apply these teachings to your everyday life, you'll discover the blessings I have described herein.

The growth you experience on your path to oneness with God will cascade into every area in your life, from your family, to your friendships, health, and career, and more. I am excited for you to progress on your path towards higher consciousness. Your divine inheritance stands ready for you to claim it.

What Spiritualism Has Taught Me

I admit that it's difficult for me to understand why some religions seem not to have evolved in their understanding of their spiritual founders' teachings over the centuries or, in some cases, thousands of years. Of course, some people have gained clear understanding of their traditions' main teachings and apply them in their lives 24/7. My comments reflect only my observations in the main. This is where I'm perplexed.

All paths lead to God. It is not difficult to honor a person who practices a different belief or follows a different religious tradition than we do. When we're led by the Higher Self, this is not difficult at all. When we are led by the Lower Self, the ego, that's when we feel the need to be right, in our own way, thus try to prove someone else wrong.

One place where I have experienced universal spirituality through honoring the common threads of truth that run through religions is at The Trail of Religion, a sculpture garden located on the historic grounds of the Indiana Association of Spiritualists in Chesterfield, Indiana. Perhaps there are other tributes that beautifully depict and honor universal spirituality and world religions, but this is one that I am aware of. In a park-like setting, The Trail of Religion is a memorial to religious leaders of the past. Although there are other spiritual leaders, past and present, among the ten statue busts featured there, we find: Abraham (Judaism), Jesus (Christianity), Muhammad (Islam),

Gautama [Buddha] (Buddhism), Zoroaster (Zoroastrianism), Lao-Tse (Taoism), Confucius (Confucianism), Vardhamana [Mahavira] (Jainism), Zeus (ancient Greece), and Osiris (ancient Egypt). Upon visiting The Trail of Religion, which was dedicated in 1943, one comes to the realization that these religious/spiritual leaders are not yours or mine; they are ours.

I find that Spiritualism accepts and embraces the truths that run through all religions. There is no dogmatic way to believe. We are each progressing on our individual soul's journey to experience whatever it is that we choose to come here to experience.

I find Spiritualism to be respectful in honoring other people's beliefs. The faith in God is strong enough to realize that God is in charge, and if a person is on a certain religious path, then he or she must be pursuing a larger purpose. Allowing and encouraging people to explore various sacred texts, spiritual principals, and beliefs, and then allowing them the freedom to choose their own beliefs is quite beautiful and respectful. Among the Spiritualists I've gathered with, as within myself, I observe no drive to "convert" someone to a particular way of believing. Perhaps we can all learn something from this underlying principle of *acceptance*.

Spiritualists believe in the basic principal of the continuity of life: that life in spirit continues on after the change called death. This basic principal is shared by most world religions of the past and present. This belief acts as a springboard propelling us in our search for higher spiritual knowledge and truth. God is Spirit, and we all live, move, and are aware of our existence as a part of this one Spirit.

It is natural for me to take the best of something, the parts that resonate with my internal guidance system—led by the Higher Self, the Divine connection—and leave the rest behind. I think it would be fair to say that not all Spiritualists share the same beliefs and perspectives that I have expressed in this book. I don't come forward as a spokesperson for Spiritualism, only to share what I have gleaned from my own experiences.

Continued Support on Your Spiritual Journey

Found in the spiritual teachings conveyed to you herein, I have offered you not only an invitation, but actual implementable guidance you can use to move yourself further along a path toward inheriting what is rightly yours.

While any individual part or chapter of this book, when studied independently, may be interesting, the true beauty comes when a person integrates the parts into a whole. This is easier to do than it may initially appear to be. Once you have set the wheels in motion, through setting a clear intention, you'll witness how Spirit begins to move in your life, arranging and re-arranging all that you need, and with perfect timing.

This message is intended to be one you refer back to from time to time, as a life manual of sorts for your path to oneness with God. You may choose to continue to use the chart you began on the seven victories in chapter 16 as a guide.

Before you close this book and set it on the shelf, I encourage you to decide how you wish to move forward. As the saying goes, "If nothing changes, then nothing changes."

In any way that I can, I would like to be a resource for you and to support you as you take your spiritual journey. This is my mission in this lifetime. You may choose to explore my continued guidance in many forms: visit me on my website, social networks, or through attending a teleclass or a public seminar or workshop. Whatever you feel drawn towards.

I have done my best, at this time, to convey to you the messages I've been inspired by Spirit to communicate. As always, I wish you, the Divine Child, only the highest and best in life and on this spiritual journey to claim your divine inheritance.

Peace be with you!

Bibliography

The Aquarian Gospel of Jesus the Christ by Levi. DeVorss & Company, 1907.

The Bhagavad Gita, translated by Eknath Easwaran. Nilgiri Press, 1985.

The Gospel of Thomas, translated by Thomas O. Lambdin, The Nag Hammadi Library general editor James M. Robinson. HarperCollins, 1990.

The Hermetica: the Lost Wisdom of the Pharaohs by Timothy Freke & Peter Gandy. Tarcher/Penguin, 1997.

The Holy Bible: From the Ancient Eastern Text, translated by George M. Lamsa. A. J. Holman Company, 1968.

The Illuminated Rumi translated by Coleman Barks. Broadway Books, 1997.

The Illustrated Book of Sacred Scriptures by Timothy Freke. Quest Books, 1998.

In Search of the Primordial Tradition & the Cosmic Christ by Father John Rossner, Ph.D. Llewellyn Publications, 1989.

Journey of Souls by Michael Newton, Ph.D. Llewellyn Publications, 1994.

The Kybalion: Hermetic Philosophy by Three Initiates. Yogi Publication Society, 1940.

Life and Teaching of the Masters of the Far East, vol.2, by Baird T. Spalding. DeVorss & Company, 1927.

Light of Consciousness Journal of Spiritual Awakening by Swami Amar Jyoti. Truth of Consciousness, 2011.

New Age Bible Interpretation: Mystery of the Christos, vol. VII, by Corinne Heline. New Age Press, 1961.

The Power of Now by Eckhart Tolle. New World Library, 1999.

Radical Forgiveness by Colin C. Tipping. Global 13 Publications, 1997.

Random House Unabridged Dictionary, second edition, Stuart Berg Flexner, Editor in Chief, 1993.

The Secret Path by Paul Brunton. E.P Dutton & Co., Inc., 1935.

The Upanishads, translated by Eknath Easwaran. Nilgiri Press, 1987.

World Scripture: A Comparative Anthology of Sacred Texts by the International Religious Foundation, edited by Andrew Wilson. Paragon House, 1991.

Resources

SPIRIT SOURCE WOULD LIKE TO be a resource for you and continue supporting you on your spiritual journey. In addition to this book, you may choose to explore additional personal and/or group spiritual guidance, coaching and support opportunities. Here are some of the ways others have benefited from on their continued journey of spiritual growth.

Live Teleclasses

We offer a regular series of live teleclasses on a wide variety of spiritual topics. You can attend these teleclasses by telephone from the comfort of your own home. To view a listing of upcoming teleclasses, go to: www.MySpiritSource.net, click on "View Events."

Special Five-part Series

At various times throughout the year, on a limited basis, we offer a Special Five-part Series. The series consists of four teleclasses of lectures, one open question and answer teleclass, and two personal one-on-one sessions. To view details and availability, go to: www. MySpiritSource.net.

One-on-one Spiritual Guidance and Support

Unlike attending a class with other people, you may prefer to have individual spiritual guidance focused specifically on your individual needs and interests. To view details of one-on-one guidance sessions, go to: www.MySpiritSource.net/one-on-one-services.php.

Workshops and Speaking Engagements

If you are interested in scheduling Michael to conduct a workshop or speaking engagement, please submit a request by email. Someone from Spirit Source will contact you regarding availability and details. Submit request to: events@MySpiritSource.net.

About the Author

REVEREND MICHAEL JONES has been involved in individual and group self-development, leadership, and coaching for over twenty-five years. His teaching style is known for shedding light on spiritual and mystical insights in a profound, focused, and clear manner. Michael is a modern-day messenger.

Michael is an ordained Spiritualist minister and founding member of Spirit Source, an organization dedicated to providing spiritual guidance to those on a path of self-discovery. It is a ministry of healing through he which he assists his spiritual brothers and sisters on their journey towards oneness with God.

Michael continues to write, teach classes, and host workshops on a variety of spiritual topics, including topics shared in this book. Michael lives in the United States.

For further information, please contact his office at:

Spirit Source
P.O. Box 8181
South Bend, IN 46660
Website: www.MySpiritSource.net
E-Mail: info@MySpiritSource.net